Your Budget Dashboard

A practical guide for managing your household budget.

Murray J. Rupert

Your Budget Dashboard
A practical guide for managing your household budget:

Copyright © 2021 Murray J. Rupert

Consulting Editor: Adriana Barbariol Rupert

All rights reserved. This includes the right to reproduce any portion of this book in any form except where expressly authorized by the author in writing.

KDP ISBN: 9798732229110

Nonfiction > Business & Economics > Budgeting
Nonfiction > Business & Economics > Personal Success

Contents

Introduction	1
The Budget Dashboard	3
Overview	5
Philosophy	7
Process	9
Bob and Janet	15
Section 1: Monthly Budgets	21
Section 2: Current Credit Card Balances	29
Section 3: Annual Recurring Expenses	33
Section 4: Annual Travel	41
Section 5: Monthly Income	43
Section 6: Savings And Investments	47
The December Budget	49
Final Thoughts	57

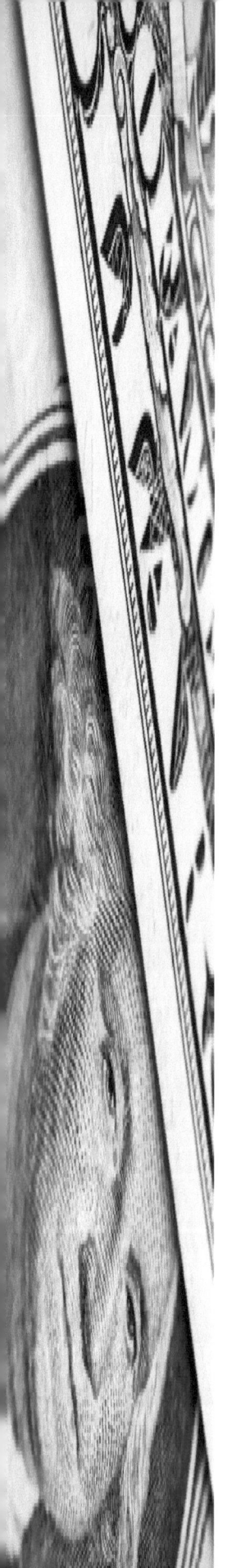

"Show me your budget, and I'll tell you what you value."
– Craig Calcaterra

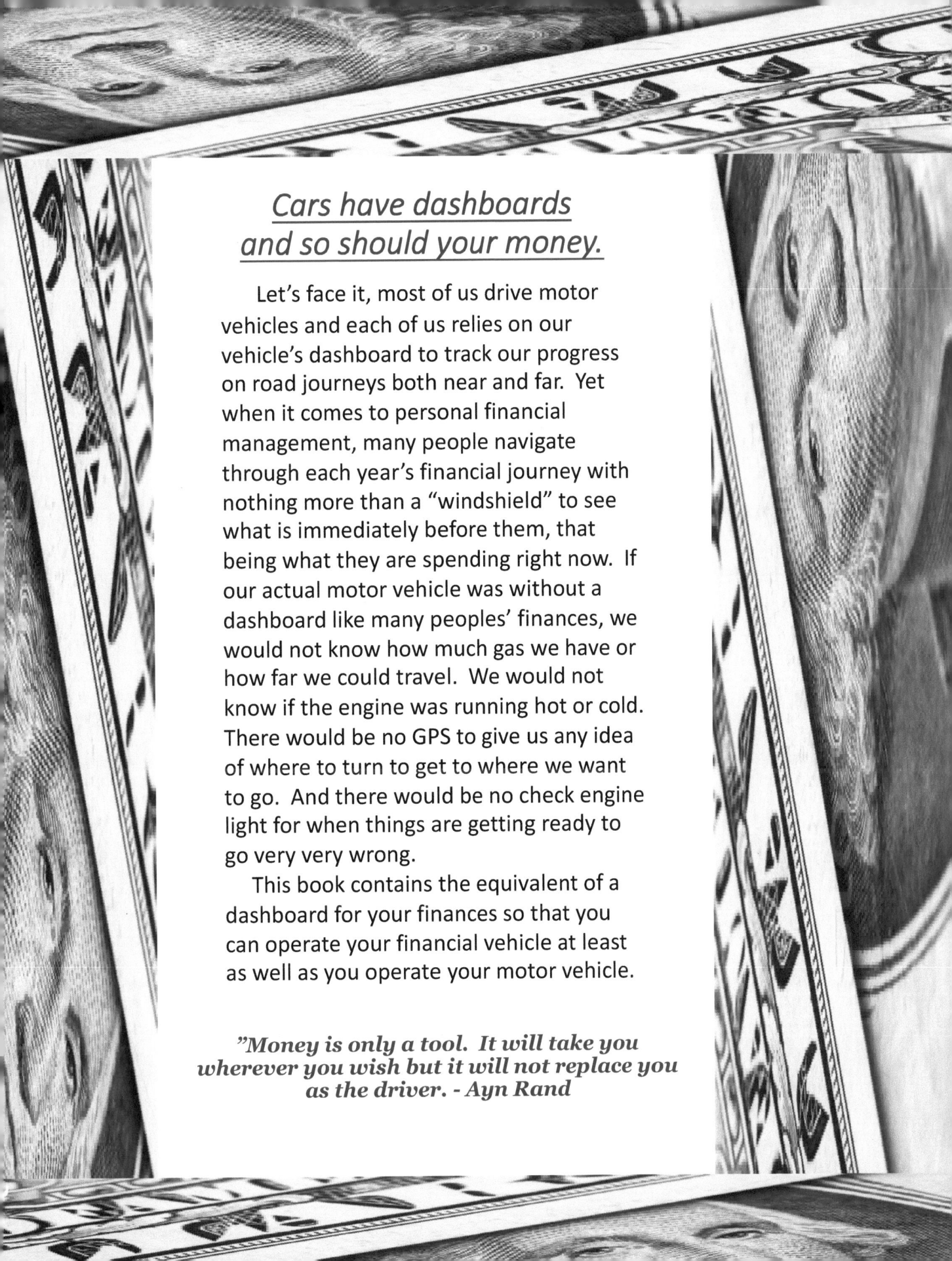

<u>Cars have dashboards and so should your money.</u>

    Let's face it, most of us drive motor vehicles and each of us relies on our vehicle's dashboard to track our progress on road journeys both near and far. Yet when it comes to personal financial management, many people navigate through each year's financial journey with nothing more than a "windshield" to see what is immediately before them, that being what they are spending right now. If our actual motor vehicle was without a dashboard like many peoples' finances, we would not know how much gas we have or how far we could travel. We would not know if the engine was running hot or cold. There would be no GPS to give us any idea of where to turn to get to where we want to go. And there would be no check engine light for when things are getting ready to go very very wrong.

    This book contains the equivalent of a dashboard for your finances so that you can operate your financial vehicle at least as well as you operate your motor vehicle.

"Money is only a tool. It will take you wherever you wish but it will not replace you as the driver. - Ayn Rand

"Money moves from those who do not manage it to those who do." - Dave Ramsey

Introduction

The Budget Dashboard which you are about to create will allow you to take complete control of your own household finances. This valuable and unique capability is a tool you can use to plan and track annual and monthly spending using an electronic line-item format tailored to your own needs.

The Budget Dashboard consists of one concise PowerPoint slide which will provide you with a one-page snapshot of your entire household budget. This format is simple to maintain and easy to synchronize with your credit card accounts and checkbook. From mortgage payments to grocery expenditures to travel funding, you will be on top of your annual and monthly spending plans.

Designed for busy people, a small investment of ten minutes per day, four times per week maintaining your dashboard will keep you on track and let you get on with your life.

Once you build your own budget dashboard from the examples provided in this guide, it will become one of your most valued tools. After all, financial knowledge is power.

"A wise person should have money in their head but not in their heart." – *Johnathan Swift*

The Budget Dashboard

Annual Budget and Spending Plan
Monthly Budget for February 202_

This page built with Microsoft Power Point

SECTION 1
Monthly Budget - $5,833.00

- Bob's Allowance – 200
- Janet's Allowance – 200
- Mortgage - 700
- Auto Loan – 350
- Home & Auto Insurance – 300
- Emergency Fund – 300
- Electric – 80
- Furnace Gas – 90
- Charity – 50
- Cell Phones –120
- Cable – 150
- Miscellaneous Expenses – 800
- Groceries – 900
- Auto Gas – 188
- Annual Recurring Expenses – 1,105
- Travel – 300

TOTAL : $5,833.00

SECTION 2
Current Credit Card Balances

- VISA (JAN Cycle) - $345.00 (Open)
- VISA (DEC Cycle) – $900.00.00 (Closed, Pay on 10 FEB)

SECTION 3
Annual Recurring Expenses

- Expenses Paid Quarterly
  - Water – 600
  - Home Association – 800

Total: $1,400.00

- Expenses Paid Semi-Annually
  - House Tax – 2,500

Total: $5,000.00

- Expenses Paid Annually:
  - Life Insurance Bob 800
  - Life Insurance Janet 650
  - Automobile Property Tax – 800
  - Credit Cards & Amazon Prime Fees – 110
  - House Maintenance - 750
  - Car Maintenance – 750
  - Medical Costs – 3,000

Total: $6,860.00

Total Annual Recurring Expenses: $13,260.00

SECTION 4
Annual Travel

Annual Total: - $3,600.00

SECTION 5
Monthly Income

- Bob's Monthly Paycheck: $2,500.00
- Janet's Monthly Paycheck: $3,333.00

Total Take Home Pay: $5,833.00

SECTION 6
Savings And Investments

- IRA – Bob - $62,000.00
- 401K Plan - Janet - $88,000.00
- Joint Savings Account – $6,500.00
- **TOTAL: $156,500.00**

Overview

The Budget Dashboard consists of one self-built electronic page divided into six sections which together provide for the annual, monthly, and daily planning and tracking of finances.

Primary inputs are monthly after-tax income or other fixed amount of funds, checks that are written, credit card charges and balances, bills paid, and savings and investment balances.

Primary outputs consist of a real-time snapshot of your personal financial status, awareness of how much money you have remaining to work with for the month and year, and the amazing financial agility that comes with this knowledge. Altogether these features facilitate a very high degree of money management confidence and sound financial decision making.

I will address some philosophy and the overall process for maintaining the Dashboard and then I will discuss each of the six sections of the Dashboard in detail, providing techniques and tips for getting the most out of your dashboard.

"The person who doesn't know where his next dollar is coming from usually doesn't know where his last dollar went." - Unknown

Annual Budget and Spending Plan
Monthly Budget for February 202_

This page built with Microsoft Power Point

SECTION 1

Monthly Budget - $5,833.00

- Bob's Allowance – 200
- Janet's Allowance – 200
- Mortgage - 700
- Auto Loan – 350
- Home & Auto Insurance – 300
- Emergency Fund – 300
- Electric – 80
- Furnace Gas – 90
- Charity – 50
- Cell Phones –120
- Cable – 150
- Miscellaneous Expenses – 800
- Groceries – 900
- Auto Gas – 188
- Annual Recurring Expenses – 1,105
- Travel – 300

TOTAL : $5,833.00

SECTION 2

Current Credit Card Balances

- VISA (JAN Cycle) - $345.00 (Open)
- VISA (DEC Cycle) – $900.00.00 (Closed, Pay on 10 FEB)

SECTION 3

Annual Recurring Expenses

- **Expenses Paid Quarterly**
    - Water – 600
    - Home Association – 800

Total: $1,400.00

- **Expenses Paid Semi-Annually**
    - House Tax – 2,500

Total: $5,000.00

- **Expenses Paid Annually:**
    - Life Insurance Bob 800
    - Life Insurance Janet 650
    - Automobile Property Tax – 800
    - Credit Cards & Amazon Prime Fees – 110
    - House Maintenance - 750
    - Car Maintenance – 750
    - Medical Costs – 3,000

Total: $6,860.00

Total Annual Recurring Expenses: $13,260.00

SECTION 4

Annual Travel

Annual Total: - $3,600.00

SECTION 5

Monthly Income

- Bob's Monthly Paycheck: $2,500.00
- Janet's Monthly Paycheck: $3,333.00

Total Take Home Pay: $5,833.00

SECTION 6

Savings And Investments

- IRA – Bob - $62,000.00
- 401K Plan - Janet - $88,000.00
- Joint Savings Account – $6,500.00
- **TOTAL: $156,500.00**

Philosophy

The Budget Dashboard is intended for people who have a burning desire to live within their income and who are willing to invest the time to track and post their spending and investment activities to the Dashboard at least several times each week. Failure to keep to this task will allow the Dashboard to become inaccurate and difficult to maintain and eventually useless. It needs to become a habit, a way of life, and the rewards for doing this will exceed most peoples' expectations as they have mine.

It is important to allocate consistent monetary resources each month to the Dashboard whether that be total take home pay or any subset of funds such as a standard amount, say for running the home, paying recurring monthly bills, grocery shopping, and filling up the cars with gas.

Finally, the Dashboard should be maintained consistently by the same person for reasons of continuity and situational awareness but should be available anytime for audit by anyone else who has an invested financial interest in it.

"The price of anything is the amount of life you exchange for it." – Henry David Thoreau

Annual Budget and Spending Plan
Monthly Budget for February 202_

This page built with Microsoft Power Point

SECTION 1
Monthly Budget - $5,833.00

- Bob's Allowance – 200
- Janet's Allowance – 200
- Mortgage - 700
- Auto Loan – 350
- Home & Auto Insurance – 300
- Emergency Fund – 300
- Electric – 80
- Furnace Gas – 90
- Charity – 50
- Cell Phones –120
- Cable – 150
- Miscellaneous Expenses – 800 (500) (50, 80, 50, 80, 100, 50, 50,)
- Groceries – 900
- Auto Gas – 188
- Annual Recurring Expenses – 1,105
- Travel = 300

TOTAL : $5,833.00

SECTION 2
Current Credit Card Balances

- **VISA (JAN Cycle) - $345.00 (Open)**
- VISA (DEC Cycle) – $900.00.00 (Closed, Pay on 10 FEB)

SECTION 3
Annual Recurring Expenses

- Expenses Paid Quarterly
  - Water – 600
  - Home Association – 800

Total: $1,400.00

- Expenses Paid Semi-Annually
  - House Tax – 2,500

Total: $5,000.00

- Expenses Paid Annually:
  - Life Insurance Bob 800
  - Life Insurance Janet 650
  - Automobile Property Tax – 800
  - Credit Cards & Amazon Prime Fees – 110
  - House Maintenance - 750
  - Car Maintenance – 750
  - Medical Costs – 3,000

Total: $6,860.00

Total Annual Recurring Expenses: $13,260.00

SECTION 4
Annual Travel

Annual Total: - $3,600.00

SECTION 5
Monthly Income

- Bob's Monthly Paycheck: $2,500.00
- Janet's Monthly Paycheck: $3,333.00

Total Take Home Pay: $5,833.00

SECTION 6
Savings And Investments

- IRA – Bob - $62,000.00
- 401K Plan - Janet - $88,000.00
- Joint Savings Account – $6,500.00
- **TOTAL: $156,500.00**

Process

Before we go any farther, let's get you up to speed on some simple but important Budget Dashboard line entry rules and terms. Look at the Miscellaneous Expenses Budget on the facing page. This budget line will have multiple entries each month because it is used to make numerous small expenditures. The 800 in black type represents the miscellaneous budget for the month. The first set of parentheses following the 800 always contains the current balance for the budget line. The current balance is usually positive and is displayed here as a green 500. This indicates that there is currently a balance of $500 on that line available to spend. The balance could also be a negative number like a red 100 which would indicate that the budget line is in the "hole" or overspent by $100 or it could just be 0. The second set of parentheses is reserved for actions which affect the balance in the first set of parentheses. I will describe each of these entries so you can see how the balance of 500 was arrived at.

The red 50 indicates that the Miscellaneous line was overspent by $50 at the end of the previous month so $50 was brought forward as a red colored debit indicating that it came from the previous month. Had the balance at the end of the previous

Annual Budget and Spending Plan
Monthly Budget for February 202_

This page built with Microsoft Power Point

SECTION 1
Monthly Budget - $5,833.00

- Bob's Allowance – 200
- Janet's Allowance – 200
- Mortgage - 700
- **Auto Loan – 350**
- Home & Auto Insurance – 300
- Emergency Fund – 300
- Electric – 80
- Furnace Gas – 90
- Charity – 50
- Cell Phones –120
- Cable – 150
- Miscellaneous Expenses – 800 (500) (50, 80, 50, 80, 100, 50, 50,)
- Groceries – 900
- Auto Gas – 188
- Annual Recurring Expenses – 1,105
- Travel – 300

TOTAL : $5,833.00

SECTION 2
Current Credit Card Balances

- VISA (JAN Cycle) - $345.00 (Open)
- VISA (DEC Cycle) – $900.00.00 (Closed, Pay on 10 FEB)

SECTION 3
Annual Recurring Expenses

- **Expenses Paid Quarterly**
  - Water – 600
  - Home Association – 800

Total: $1,400.00

- **Expenses Paid Semi-Annually**
  - House Tax – 2,500

Total: $5,000.00

- **Expenses Paid Annually:**
  - Life Insurance Bob 800
  - Life Insurance Janet 650
  - Automobile Property Tax – 800
  - Credit Cards & Amazon Prime Fees – 110
  - House Maintenance - 750
  - Car Maintenance – 750
  - Medical Costs – 3,000

Total: $6,860.00

Total Annual Recurring Expenses: $13,260.00

SECTION 4
Annual Travel

Annual Total: - $3,600.00

SECTION 5
Monthly Income

- **Bob's Monthly Paycheck: $2,500.00**
- **Janet's Monthly Paycheck: $3,333.00**

Total Take Home Pay: $5,833.00

SECTION 6
Savings And Investments

- **IRA – Bob - $62,000.00**
- **401K Plan - Janet - $88,000.00**
- **Joint Savings Account – $6,500.00**
- **TOTAL: $156,500.00**

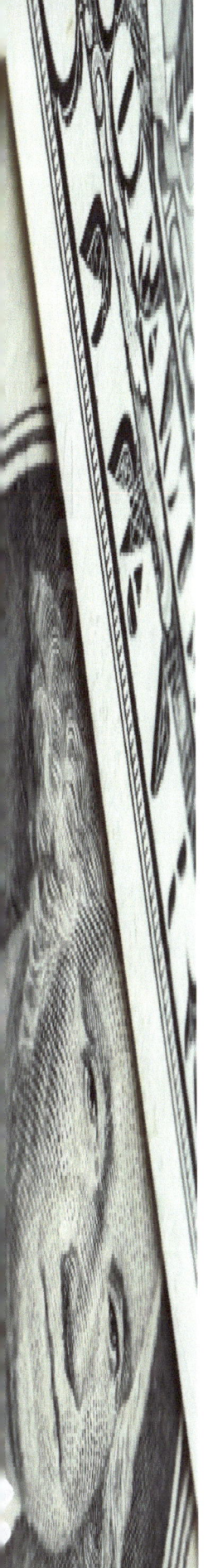

month been positive, a green colored number would have been brought forward. The first 80 in black was a credit charge for Amazon which posted to the credit card account on-line. The 50 in black is a $50 check that was written to cover a parking ticket. The second 80 in green is a credit card account credit from Amazon for that previous $80 Amazon charge where the product was later sent back as defective. The black 100 is a $100 charge for books purchased for night courses at the community college. Next, $50 was charged for a new mattress pad, and finally, a check was written for $50 to cover professional dues for the year. And that gets us to the current balance of 500. All Dashboard lines having multiple entries will be maintained in this way using this color scheme. Most dollar signs within the Dashboard are dropped to save space.

Single-entry Dashboard lines are easier to maintain than multiple entry lines. These lines are paid once each month. Two examples of single-entry lines on the facing page are first, the Auto Loan for $350 which is paid every month around the 10th. This payment has been debited by the bank from checking and is now paid so this line has been **bolded** to indicate that the auto loan has been paid for the month. The second example is the Mortgage bill which will not be paid until the 20th of the month so it has not been bolded. Single-entry lines in Section 1 need no parentheses for balances or actions which affect balances. Once the bill is paid, it is highlighted in **bold** type.

Annual Budget and Spending Plan
Monthly Budget for February 202_

This page built with Microsoft Power Point

SECTION 1
Monthly Budget - $5,833.00

- Bob's Allowance – 200
- Janet's Allowance – 200
- Mortgage - 700
- Auto Loan – 350
- Home & Auto Insurance – 300
- Emergency Fund – 300
- Electric – 80
- Furnace Gas – 90
- Charity – 50
- Cell Phones –120
- Cable – 150
- Miscellaneous Expenses – 800 (500) 50, 80, 50, 80, 100, 50, 50,)
- Groceries – 900
- Auto Gas – 188
- Annual Recurring Expenses – 1,105
- Travel = 300

TOTAL : $5,833.00

SECTION 2
Current Credit Card Balances

- VISA (JAN Cycle) - $345.00 (Open)
- VISA (DEC Cycle) – $900.00.00 (Closed, Pay on 10 FEB)

SECTION 3
Annual Recurring Expenses

- Expenses Paid Quarterly
  - Water – 600
  - Home Association – 800

Total: $1,400.00

- Expenses Paid Semi-Annually
  - House Tax – 2,500

Total: $5,000.00

- Expenses Paid Annually:
  - Life Insurance Bob 800
  - Life Insurance Janet 650
  - Automobile Property Tax – 800
  - Credit Cards & Amazon Prime Fees – 110
  - House Maintenance – 750
  - Car Maintenance – 750
  - Medical Costs – 3,000

Total: $6,860.00

Total Annual Recurring Expenses: $13,260.00

SECTION 4
Annual Travel

Annual Total: - $3,600.00

SECTION 5
Monthly Income

- Bob's Monthly Paycheck: $2,500.00
- Janet's Monthly Paycheck: $3,333.00

Total Take Home Pay: $5,833.00

SECTION 6
Savings And Investments

- IRA – Bob - $62,000.00
- 401K Plan - Janet - $88,000.00
- Joint Savings Account – $6,500.00
- **TOTAL: $156,500.00**

As we proceed, the terms budget dashboard, budget, and dashboard are used interchangeably for the sake of variety and flexibility but will have the same meaning as Budget Dashboard. The term mortgage will also refer to rent for those who do not own their current residence.

> *"You must gain control of your money or or the lack of it will forever control you." – Dave Ramsey*

Annual Budget and Spending Plan
Monthly Budget for February 202_

This page built with Microsoft Power Point

SECTION 1

Monthly Budget - $5,833.00

- Bob's Allowance – 200 (200) (,)
- Janet's Allowance – 200 (200) (,)
- Mortgage - 700
- Auto Loan – 350
- Home & Auto Insurance – 300
- Emergency Fund – 300 (300) (,)
- Electric – 80
- Furnace Gas – 90
- Charity – 50 (50) (,)
- Cell Phones –120
- Cable – 150
- Miscellaneous Expenses – 800 (800) ()
- Groceries – 900 (900) (,)
- Auto Gas – 188 (188) (,)
- Annual Recurring Expenses – 1,105 (1,105) (,)
- Travel – 300 (300) (,)

TOTAL : $5,833.00 ($5,833.00)

SECTION 2

Current Credit Card Balances

- **VISA (JAN Cycle) - $345.00 (Open)**
- VISA (DEC Cycle) – $900.00.00 (Closed, Pay on 10 FEB)

SECTION 3

Annual Recurring Expenses

- **Expenses Paid Quarterly**
  - Water – 600 (600) () (JAN, APR, JUL, OCT)
  - Home Association – 800 (800) () (JAN, APR, JUL, OCT)

Total: $1,400.00 (1,400.00)

- **Expenses Paid Semi-Annually**
  - House Tax – 2,500 (JUL/DEC)

Total: $5,000.00 ($5,000.00)

- **Expenses Paid Annually:**
  - Life Insurance Bob 800 (Due JUL)
  - Life Insurance Janet 650 (Due NOV)
  - Automobile Property Tax – 800 (800) (Due OCT)
  - Credit Cards & Amazon Prime Fees – 110 (110) ()
  - House Maintenance - 750 (750) ()
  - Car Maintenance – 750 (750) ()
  - Medical Costs – 3,000 (3,000) ()

Total: $6,870.00 ($6,860.00)

Total Annual Recurring Expenses: $13,260.00 ($13,260.00)

SECTION 4

Annual Travel

Annual Total: - $3,600.00 ($3,600) ()

SECTION 5

Monthly Income

- Bob's Monthly Paycheck: $2,500.00
- Janet's Monthly Paycheck: $3,333.00

Total Take Home Pay: $5,833.00

SECTION 6

Savings And Investments

- IRA – Bob - $62,000.00
- 401K Plan - Janet - $88,000.00
- Joint Savings Account – $6,500.00
- **TOTAL: $156,500.00**

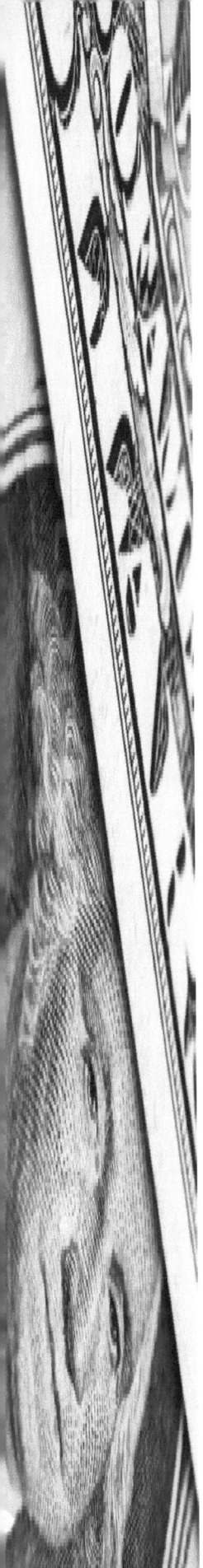

Bob And Janet

The Budget Dashboard example on the facing page represents a hypothetical budget for a couple who we will call Bob and Janet. Janet maintains the dashboard but consults regularly with Bob on its status, sometimes even printing off the Dashboard page and discussing it with him at dinnertime.

Bob and Janet elected to place their combined monthly disposable income (Section 5) from their respective employments under Janet's management as the keeper of the Dashboard.

When either Bob or Janet write a check from the joint checking account for any reason, Janet goes to the appropriate budget line in the Dashboard and enters it as a debit.

When a credit card charge status on-line changes from pending to paid, Janet also goes to the appropriate budget line in the Dashboard and enters it as a debit. If there happens to be a credit refund on-line, Janet will credit that amount back to the appropriate Budget Dashboard line using green numbers to indicate a credit. Every time Janet works with credit card information, she also updates the Current Open Credit Card Balance in Section 2. Keeping the Current Credit Card Balances up-to-date is important because those balances must be accounted for with funds-on-hand in the joint checking account.

Annual Budget and Spending Plan
Monthly Budget for February 202_

This page built with Microsoft Power Point

SECTION 1
Monthly Budget - $5,833.00

- Bob's Allowance – 200 (200) ()
- Janet's Allowance – 200 (200) ()
- Mortgage – 700
- Auto Loan – 350
- Home & Auto Insurance – 300
- Emergency Fund – 300 (300) ()
- Electric – 80
- Furnace Gas – 90
- Charity – 50 (50) ()
- Cell Phones – 120
- Cable – 150
- Miscellaneous Expenses – 800 (800) ()
- Groceries – 900 (900) ()
- Auto Gas – 188 (188)
- Annual Recurring Expenses – 1,105 (1,105) ()
- Travel – 300 (300) ()

TOTAL: $5,833.00 ($5,833.00)

SECTION 2
Current Credit Card Balances

- VISA (JAN Cycle) - $345.00 (Open)
- VISA (DEC Cycle) – $900.00.00 (Closed, Pay on 10 FEB)

SECTION 3
Annual Recurring Expenses

- Expenses Paid Quarterly
  - Water – 600 (600) (JAN, APR, JUL, OCT)
  - Home Association – 800 (800) (JAN, APR, JUL, OCT)

Total: $1,400.00 (1,400.00)

- Expenses Paid Semi-Annually
  - House Tax – 2,500 (JUL/DEC)

Total: $5,000.00 ($5,000.00)

- Expenses Paid Annually:
  - Life Insurance Bob 800 (Due JUL)
  - Life Insurance Janet 650 (Due NOV)
  - Automobile Property Tax – 800 (800) (Due OCT)
  - Credit Cards & Amazon Prime Fees – 110 (110) ()
  - House Maintenance – 750 (750) ()
  - Car Maintenance – 750 (750) ()
  - Medical Costs – 3,000 (3,000) ()

Total: $6,870.00 ($6,860.00)

Total Annual Recurring Expenses: $13,260.00 ($13,260.00)

SECTION 4
Annual Travel

Annual Total: - $3,600.00 ($3,600) ()

SECTION 5
Monthly Income

- Bob's Monthly Paycheck: $2,500.00
- Janet's Monthly Paycheck: $3,333.00
- Total Take Home Pay: $5,833.00

SECTION 6
Savings And Investments

- IRA – Bob - $62,000.00
- 401K Plan - Janet - $88,000.00
- Joint Savings Account – $6,500.00
- TOTAL: $156,500.00

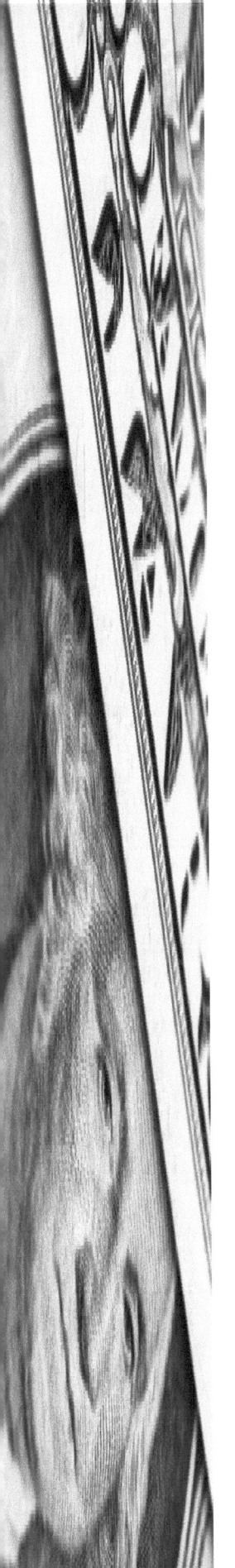

Debiting both the checks written and credit card expenditures in a timely manner within the Dashboard line entries makes certain that all monthly expenses will be covered by the funds in the joint checking account so that the credit card balance can be paid in full when due. Of course, Bob and Janet like everyone else will sometimes spend more than they have for the month. When this happens, the balance on a Budget Dashboard line will turn red, indicating that there is a deficit on that line. Bob and Janet will then have to find a way to make this up either by transferring money from a more robust budget line or by carrying the negative balance forward to next month. For example, if the Grocery line is in the hole at the end of the month by $100 and there is $50 left over on the Gas line and $50 left over on the Miscellaneous line, then Janet can transfer those amounts to the Grocery line to bring it to $0 for the month and get it out of the red.

One thing that Bob and Janet try not to do is "raid" their accumulated balances on their Annual Recurring Expenses or Annual Travel budget lines and use them to balance other lines which may be short on funds. They know that doing this tends to just kick the problem down the road and will throw their future travel plans and annual recurring expense payments out of balance. What they decided was that if they could not cross-level among the other monthly Dashboard lines, they will

Annual Budget and Spending Plan
Monthly Budget for February 202_

This page built with Microsoft Power Point

SECTION 1

Monthly Budget - $5,833.00

- Bob's Allowance – 200 (200) (,)
- Janet's Allowance – 200 (200) (,)
- Mortgage - 700
- Auto Loan – 350
- Home & Auto Insurance – 300
- Emergency Fund – 300 (300) (,)
- Electric – 80
- Furnace Gas – 90
- Charity – 50 (50) (,)
- Cell Phones –120
- Cable – 150
- Miscellaneous Expenses – 800 (800) ( )
- Groceries – 900 (900) (,)
- Auto Gas – 188 (188) (,)
- Annual Recurring Expenses – 1,105 (1,105) (,)
- Travel – 300 (300) (,)

TOTAL : $5,833.00 ($5,833.00)

SECTION 2

Current Credit Card Balances

- VISA (JAN Cycle) - $345.00 (Open)
- VISA (DEC Cycle) – $900.00.00 (Closed, Pay on 10 FEB)

SECTION 3

Annual Recurring Expenses

- **Expenses Paid Quarterly**
  - Water – 600 (600) () (JAN, APR, JUL, OCT)
  - Home Association – 800 (800) () (JAN, APR, JUL, OCT)

Total: $1,400.00 (1,400.00)

- **Expenses Paid Semi-Annually**
  - House Tax – 2,500 (JUL/DEC)

Total: $5,000.00 ($5,000.00)

- **Expenses Paid Annually:**
  - Life Insurance Bob 800 (Due JUL)
  - Life Insurance Janet 650 (Due NOV)
  - Automobile Property Tax – 800 (800) (Due OCT)
  - Credit Cards & Amazon Prime Fees – 110 (110) ( )
  - House Maintenance - 750 (750) ( )
  - Car Maintenance – 750 (750) ( )
  - Medical Costs – 3,000 (3,000) ( )

Total: $6,860.00 ($6,860.00)

Total Annual Recurring Expenses: $13,260.00 ($13,260.00)

SECTION 4

Annual Travel

Annual Total: - $3,600.00 ($3,600) ()

SECTION 5

Monthly Income

- Bob's Monthly Paycheck: $2,500.00
- Janet's Monthly Paycheck: $3,333.00

Total Take Home Pay: $5,833.00

SECTION 6

Savings And Investments

- IRA – Bob - $62,000.00
- 401K Plan - Janet - $88,000.00
- Joint Savings Account – $6,500.00
- TOTAL: $156,500.00

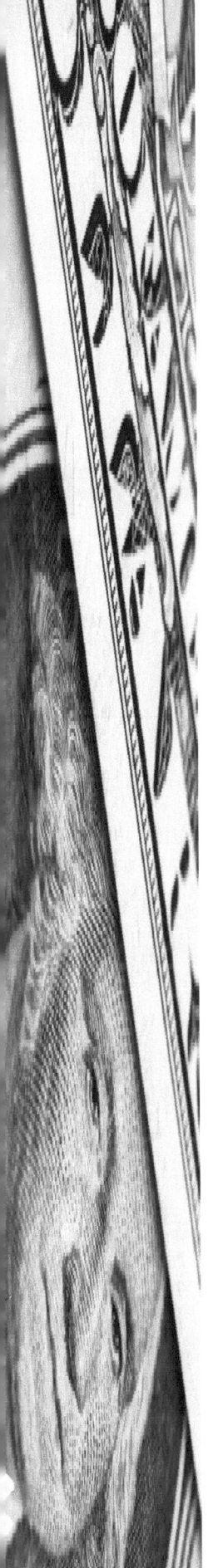

either use funds from the Emergency Fund line or they will transfer some money into joint checking from savings to keep the budget in balance. In some cases, they will just carry a small negative balance over to the next month. This has worked well for them so far. Bob and Janet feel good when the budget ends the month at $0 or better across all monthly Budget Dashboard lines.

Now it is time to move on to maintaining the Dashboard lines. In the following pages, we will see how to maintain individual Dashboard lines by Section.

"A simple fact that is hard to learn is that the time to save money is when you have some" – Joe Moore

Annual Budget and Spending Plan
Monthly Budget for February 202_

This page built with Microsoft Power Point

SECTION 1
Monthly Budget - $5,833.00

- Bob's Allowance – 200
- Janet's Allowance – 200
- Mortgage – 700
- Auto Loan – 350
- Home & Auto Insurance – 300
- Emergency Fund – 300
- Electric – 80
- Natural Gas – 90
- Charity – 50
- Cell Phones – 120
- Cable – 150
- Miscellaneous Expenses – 800
- Groceries – 900
- Auto Gas – 188
- Annual Recurring Expenses – 1,105
- Travel – 300

TOTAL: $5,833.00

SECTION 2
Current Credit Card Balances

- VISA (JAN Cycle) - $345.00 (Open)
- VISA (DEC Cycle) = $900.00.00 (Closed, Pay on 10 FEB)

SECTION 3
Annual Recurring Expenses

- Expenses Paid Quarterly
  - Water – 600 (JAN, APR, JUL, OCT)
  - Home Association – 800 (JAN, APR, JUL, OCT)

Total: $1,400.00

- Expenses Paid Semi-Annually
  - House Tax – 2,500 (JUL/DEC)

Total: $5,000.00 If not paid with mortgage.

- Expenses Paid Annually:
  - Life Insurance Bob 800 (JUL)
  - Life Insurance Janet 650 (NOV)
  - Automobile Property Tax – 800 (OCT)
  - Credit Cards & Amazon Prime Fees – 120
  - House Maintenance – 750
  - Car Maintenance – 750
  - Medical Costs – 3,000

Total: $6,860.00

Total Annual Recurring Expenses: $13,260.00

SECTION 4
Annual Travel

Annual Total: - $3,600.00

SECTION 5
Monthly Income

- Bob's Monthly Paycheck: $2,500.00
- Janet's Monthly Paycheck: $3,333.00
- Total Take Home Pay: $5,833.00

SECTION 6
Savings And Investments

- IRA – Bob - $62,000.00
- 401K Plan - Janet - $88,000.00
- Joint Savings Account – $6,500.00
- **TOTAL: $156,500.00**

Section 1: Monthly Budget

(1) Section 1 displays budget lines which cover monthly expenditures that account for all take home pay for Bob and Janet. In our example budget, that take home pay amount is listed in the title line for Section 1 as $5,833.00 which matches the total take home pay in Section 5. All budget lines in Section 1 should add up to the Total Take Home Pay in Section 5.

(2) An allowance for each spouse to spend as they choose eliminates a host of issues that may arise. Bob and Alice have a rule that they cannot even question what the other does with their allowance although they often chip in to cover meals out together.

(3) The Emergency Fund budget line is an accumulating line which grows each month. An emergency fund is a great idea because there are few things so frequent in life as unexpected financial emergencies. Left to grow every month it will be there when it is needed.

(4) Miscellaneous Expenses are for those smaller needs that pop up during the month. These pop ups do not include monthly or other recurring bills, food, gas or eating out.

(5) The Groceries budget line, covers the cost of the food purchased for eating at home and does not include dining out although that can always be broken out into a separate category.

Annual Budget and Spending Plan
Monthly Budget for February 202_

This page built with Microsoft Power Point

SECTION 1
Monthly Budget - $5,833.00

①
② - Bob's Allowance – 200
    - Janet's Allowance – 200
    - Mortgage - 700
    - Auto Loan – 350
    - Home & Auto Insurance – 300
③ - Emergency Fund – 300
    - Electric – 80
    - Natural Gas – 90
    - Charity – 50
    - Cell Phones –120
    - Cable – 150
④ - Miscellaneous Expenses – 800
⑤ - Groceries – 900
    - Auto Gas – 188
⑥ - Annual Recurring Expenses – 1,105
⑦ - Travel – 300

⑧ **TOTAL : $5,833.00**

SECTION 2
Current Credit Card Balances

- **VISA (JAN Cycle) - $345.00 (Open)**
- VISA (DEC Cycle) – $900.00.00 (Closed, Pay on 10 FEB)

SECTION 3
Annual Recurring Expenses

- **Expenses Paid Quarterly**
    - Water – 600 (JAN, APR, JUL, OCT)
    - Home Association – 800 (JAN, APR, JUL, OCT)

Total: $1,400.00

- **Expenses Paid Semi-Annually**
    - House Tax – 2,500 (JUL/DEC)

Total: $5,000.00 If not paid with mortgage.

- **Expenses Paid Annually:**
    - Life Insurance Bob 800 (JUL)
    - Life Insurance Janet 650 (NOV)
    - Automobile Property Tax – 800 (OCT)
    - Credit Cards & Amazon Prime Fees – 120
    - House Maintenance - 750
    - Car Maintenance – 750
    - Medical Costs – 3,000

Total: $6,860.00

Total Annual Recurring Expenses: $13,260.00

SECTION 4
Annual Travel

Annual Total: - $3,600.00

SECTION 5
Monthly Income

- **Bob's Monthly Paycheck: $2,500.00**
- **Janet's Monthly Paycheck: $3,333.00**

Total Take Home Pay: $5,833.00

SECTION 6
Savings And Investments

- **IRA – Bob - $62,000.00**
- **401K Plan - Janet - $88,000.00**
- **Joint Savings Account – $6,500.00**
- **TOTAL: $156,500.00**

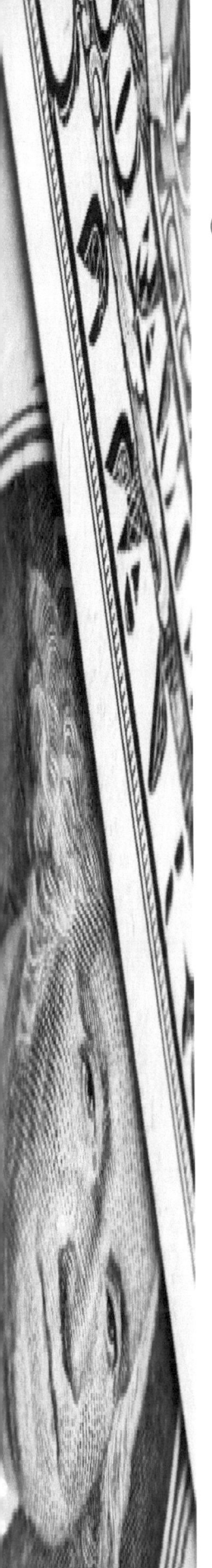

(6) The Annual Recurring Expense budget line is an accumulating line which grows monthly and funds Section 3 which contains all major annual recurring expenses. This budget line creates financial calm by having money available for those expenses as they come due.

(7) The Travel budget line is also an accumulating line which grows monthly and funds Section 4 which is the Annual Travel Budget. Again, saving some funds each month will make travel less stressful by making certain that at least part of travel is funded when it occurs.

(8) The TOTAL, is a roll-up of the funds allocated to the budget for the month and reflects how much money is added to checking each month to cover these monthly expenditures.

> *"Too many people spend money they haven't earned, to buy things they don't want, to impress people that they don't like." — Will Rogers*

Annual Budget and Spending Plan
Monthly Budget for February 202_

This page built with Microsoft Power Point

SECTION 1
Monthly Budget - $5,833.00

1. Bob's Allowance – 200 ( ) (, 25 Split dining out, 15 new wallet, 29 golf balls, 80 ATM,)
2. Janet's Allowance – 200 (120) (15, 25 split, 6, 11, 23,)
3. Mortgage – 700
4. Auto Loan – 350
5. Home & Auto Insurance – 300
6. Emergency Fund – 300 (600) (300,)
7. Electric – 80
8. Natural Gas – 90
9. Charity – 50 (40) (10,)
10. Cell Phones – 120
11. Cable – 150
12. Miscellaneous Expenses – 800 (751) (49 crock pot,)
13. Groceries – 900 (650) (250,)
14. Auto Gas – 188 (188) ( )
15. Annual Recurring Expenses – 1,105 (1,660) (755, 50 car service, 150 prescription drugs,)
16. Travel – 300 (600) (300,)

TOTAL : $5,833.00 ($5,520.00)

SECTION 2
Current Credit Card Balances

- VISA (JAN Cycle) - $345.00 (Open)
- VISA (DEC Cycle) – $900.00.00 (Closed, Pay on 10 FEB)

SECTION 3
Annual Recurring Expenses

- Expenses Paid Quarterly
    - Water – 600 (450) (150,) (JAN, APR, JUL, OCT)
    - Home Association – 800 (600) (200,) (JAN, APR, JUL, OCT)

Total: $1,400.00 ($1,050.00)

- Expenses Paid Semi-Annually
    - House Tax – 2,500 (JUL/DEC)

Total: $5,000.00 ($5,000.00) If not paid with mortgage.

- Expenses Paid Annually:
    - Life Insurance Bob 800 (Due JUL)
    - Life Insurance Janet 650 (Due NOV)
    - Automobile Property Tax – 800 (800) (Due OCT)
    - Credit Cards & Amazon Prime Fees – 120 (120) ( )
    - House Maintenance – 750 (740) ( )
    - Car Maintenance – 750 (700) (50,)
    - Medical Costs – 3,000 (2,850) (150;)

Total: $6,860.00 ($6,660.00)

Total Annual Recurring Expenses: $13,260.00 ($12,710.00)

SECTION 4
Annual Travel

Annual Total: - $3,600.00 ($3,600) ()

SECTION 5
Monthly Income

- Bob's Monthly Paycheck: $2,500.00
- Janet's Monthly Paycheck: $3,333.00
- Total Take Home Pay: $5,833.00

SECTION 6
Savings And Investments

- IRA – Bob - $62,000.00
- 401K Plan - Janet - $88,000.00
- Joint Savings Account – $6,500.00
- TOTAL: $156,500.00

1. It is now the second week of February. This budget line shows that Bob has a $200 allowance of which he has a balance of $61 remaining (first set of parentheses). The second set of parentheses show that Bob brought a surplus of $10 forward from January, that he split a meal out with Janet, and that he purchased a new wallet, golf balls, and made an ATM withdrawal. Bob likes details so each of his purchases is listed after the cost.

2. Janet has $120 remaining of her allowance. The budget line shows that Janet was $15 in the hole at the end of January. This negative amount was brought forward and deducted from her starting balance. Also reflected is the split meal out with Bob and other purchases of $6, $11, and $23. Janet does not post the details of her purchases.

3. The Mortgage budget line is now "**bold**", reflecting that it has been paid.

4. The Emergency fund budget line has grown to $600 because nothing was spent in January so $300 was brought forward.

5. Janet put a check for $10 in the collection basket at Church this past Sunday.

6. The Miscellaneous budget line shows a current balance of $751 after the purchase of a new crock pot.

7. Saturday's trip to the grocery store resulted in a credit card charge of $250. The Grocery budget line now shows a remaining balance for the month of $650.

Annual Budget and Spending Plan
Monthly Budget for February 202_

This page built with Microsoft Power Point

SECTION 1

Monthly Budget - $5,833.00

1. - Bob's Allowance – 200 (61) (10, 25 Split dining out, 15 new wallet, 29 golf balls, 80 ATM,)
2. - Janet's Allowance – 200 (120) (15, 25 split, 6, 11, 23,)
3. - **Mortgage - 700**
   - Auto Loan – 350
   - Home & Auto Insurance – 300
4. - Emergency Fund – 300 (600) (300,)
   - Electric – 80
   - **Natural Gas – 90**
5. - Charity – 50 (40) (10,)
   - Cell Phones –120
   - **Cable – 150**
6. - Miscellaneous Expenses – 800 (751) (49 crock pot,)
7. - Groceries – 900 (650) (250,)
   - Auto Gas – 188 (188) (,)
8. - Annual Recurring Expenses – 1,105 (1,660) (755, 50 car service, 150 prescription drugs,)
9. - **Travel – 300 (600) (300,)**

10. TOTAL : $5,833.00 ($5,920.00)

SECTION 2

Current Credit Card Balances

- VISA (JAN Cycle) - $345.00 (Open)
- VISA (DEC Cycle) – $900.00.00 (Closed, Pay on 10 FEB)

SECTION 3

Annual Recurring Expenses

- **Expenses Paid Quarterly**
  - Water – 600 (450) (150,) (JAN, APR, JUL, OCT)
  - Home Association – 800 (600) (200,) (JAN, APR, JUL, OCT)

Total: **$1,400.00** (1,050.00)

- **Expenses Paid Semi-Annually**
  - House Tax – 2,500 (JUL/DEC)

Total: **$5,000.00** ($5,000.00) If not paid with mortgage.

- **Expenses Paid Annually:**
  - Life Insurance Bob 800 (Due JUL)
  - Life Insurance Janet 650 (Due NOV)
  - Automobile Property Tax – 800 (800) (Due OCT)
  - Credit Cards & Amazon Prime Fees – 120 (120) ( )
  - House Maintenance - 750 (740) ( )
  - Car Maintenance – 750 (700) (50,)
  - Medical Costs – 3,000 (2,850) (150,)

Total: **$6,860.00** ($6,660.00)

Total Annual Recurring Expenses: $13,260.00 ($12,710.00)

SECTION 4

Annual Travel

Annual Total: - $3,600.00 ($3,600) ()

SECTION 5

Monthly Income

- **Bob's Monthly Paycheck: $2,500.00**
- **Janet's Monthly Paycheck: $3,333.00**
- **Total Take Home Pay: $5,833.00**

SECTION 6

Savings And Investments

- **IRA – Bob - $62,000.00**
- **401K Plan - Janet - $88,000.00**
- **Joint Savings Account – $6,500.00**
- **TOTAL: $156,500.00**

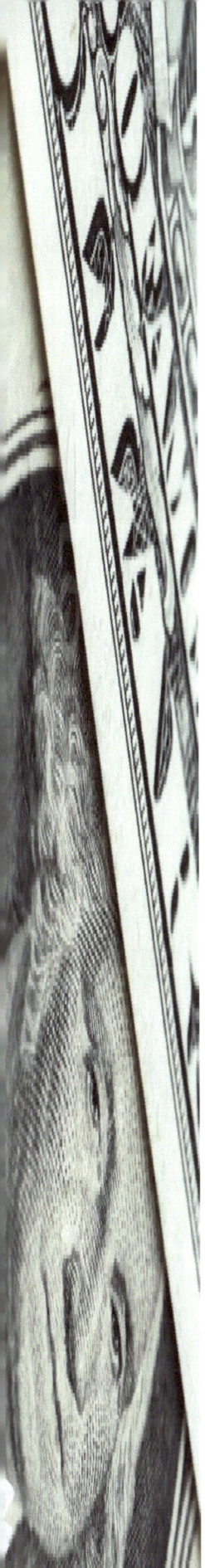

⑧ The Annual Recurring Expenses budget line shows a current balance of $1,660. Only $755 was brought forward from January because Janet sent out checks last month to pay both quarterly bills for water and the homeowners association (also reflected in Section 3). So far in February, there have been bills for a service on the SUV and for prescription drugs (also reflected in Section 3).

⑨ The Travel budget line has now accrued to $600 after $300 was rolled over from January. No family travel is scheduled until June so it is now "**bold**" because no more activity is expected this month.

⑩ The TOTAL line shows a remaining unspent balance in the budget this month of $5,520. This balance is the sum of the "green" balances on each line that has a green balance plus any monthly bill which has not yet been paid. For example, there is $40 remaining in charity and the cell phone bill for $120 has yet to be paid. Lines which are in **bold, like the cable bill,** have already been paid and are no longer counted in the "green" balance. This balance will be important later when the Dashboard and joint checking account are reconciled.

> *"There is no dignity quite so impressive, and no independence quite so important, as living within your means." — Calvin Coolidge*

Annual Budget and Spending Plan
Monthly Budget for February 202_

This page built with Microsoft Power Point

SECTION 1
Monthly Budget - $5,833.00

- Bob's Allowance – 200 ( ) (, 25 Split dining out, 15 new wallet, 25 golf balls, 80 ATM,)
- Janet's Allowance – 200 (120) (15, 25 split, 6, 11, 23,)
- Mortgage – 700
- Auto Loan – 350
- Home & Auto Insurance – 300
- Emergency Fund – 300 (600) (300,)
- Electric – 80
- Natural Gas – 90
- Charity – 50 (40) (10,)
- Cell Phones – 120
- Cable – 150
- Miscellaneous Expenses – 800 (751) (49 crock pot,)
- Groceries – 900 (650) (250,)
- Auto Gas – 188 (188)
- Annual Recurring Expenses – 1,105 (1,660) (755, 50 car service, 150 Med Supplement,)
- Travel – 300 (600) (300,)

TOTAL : $5,833.00 ($5,520.00)

SECTION 2
Current Credit Card Balances

- VISA (JAN Cycle) - $345.00 (Open)
- VISA (DEC Cycle) – $900.00.00 (Closed, Pay on 10 FEB)

SECTION 3
Annual Recurring Expenses

- Expenses Paid Quarterly
  - Water – 600 (450) (150,) (JAN, APR, JUL, OCT)
  - Home Association – 800 (600) (200,) (JAN, APR, JUL, OCT)

Total: $1,400.00 (1,050.00)

- Expenses Paid Semi-Annually
  - House Tax – 2,500 (JUL/DEC)

Total: $5,000.00 ($5,000.00) If not paid with mortgage.

- Expenses Paid Annually:
  - Life Insurance Bob 800 (Due JUL)
  - Life Insurance Janet 650 (Due NOV)
  - Automobile Property Tax – 800 (800) (Due OCT)
  - Credit Cards & Amazon Prime Fees – 120 (120) ( )
  - House Maintenance - 750 (740) ( )
  - Car Maintenance – 750 (700) (50,)
  - Medical Costs – 3,000 (2,850) (150,)

Total: $6,860.00 ($6,660.00)

Total Annual Recurring Expenses: $13,260.00 ($12,710.00)

SECTION 4
Annual Travel

Annual Total: - $3,600.00 ($3,600) ()

SECTION 5
Monthly Income

- Bob's Monthly Paycheck: $2,500.00
- Janet's Monthly Paycheck: $3,333.00

Total Take Home Pay: $5,833.00

SECTION 6
Savings And Investments

- IRA – Bob - $62,000.00
- 401K Plan - Janet - $88,000.00
- Joint Savings Account – $6,500.00
- TOTAL: $156,500.00

Section 2: Current Credit Card Balances

Bob and Janet share a VISA credit card by which they can accumulate airline miles to augment their travel budget. They try to pay as many bills as possible with this card and use it for just about all their purchasing needs. They also pay this card off every month because it is fully supported by their Budget Dashboard entries. By managing their money this way, Bob and Janet accumulate lots of airline miles and never pay a penny of interest on their credit card balance. This makes them great money managers who are living within their means.

Janet monitors the credit card account on-line several times each week. When she signs into the account on-line, she reviews both pending charges and posted charges to make certain that they are the only people using their card. Once she is comfortable, Janet looks at the current credit card balance and then subtracts the previous open balance that is on the Dashboard from it. This will give Janet the sum of all new charges. She then works her way through the new posted charges (not pending charges), adding them until she arrives at a figure representing the sum of all the new charges. Once Janet is certain she knows what those new charges are, she moves on to the next step.

Annual Budget and Spending Plan
Monthly Budget for February 202_

This page built with Microsoft Power Point

SECTION 1

Monthly Budget - $5,833.00

- Bob's Allowance – 200 (61) (10, 25 Split dining out, 15 new wallet, 29 golf balls, 80 ATM,)
- Janet's Allowance – 200 (120) (15, 25 split, 6, 11, 23,)
- **Mortgage - 700**
- Auto Loan – 350
- Home & Auto Insurance – 300
- Emergency Fund – 300 (600) (300,)
- Electric – 80
- **Natural Gas – 90**
- Charity – 50 (40) (10,)
- Cell Phones –120
- **Cable – 150**
- Miscellaneous Expenses – 800 (751) (49 crock pot,)
- Groceries – 900 (650) (250,)
- Auto Gas – 188 (188) (,)
- Annual Recurring Expenses – 1,105 (1,660) (755, 50 car service, 150 Med Supplement,)
- **Travel – 300** (600) (300,)

TOTAL : $5,833.00 ($5,520.00)

SECTION 2

Current Credit Card Balances

- VISA (JAN Cycle) - $345.00 (Open)
- VISA (DEC Cycle) – $900.00.00 (Closed, Pay on 10 FEB)

SECTION 3

Annual Recurring Expenses

- **Expenses Paid Quarterly**
  - Water – 600 (450) (150,) (JAN, APR, JUL, OCT)
  - Home Association – 800 (600) (200,) (JAN, APR, JUL, OCT)

Total: $1,400.00 (1,050.00)

- **Expenses Paid Semi-Annually**
  - House Tax – 2,500 (JUL/DEC)

Total: $5,000.00 ($5,000.00) If not paid with mortgage.

- **Expenses Paid Annually:**
  - Life Insurance Bob 800 (Due JUL)
  - Life Insurance Janet 650 (Due NOV)
  - Automobile Property Tax – 800 (800) (Due OCT)
  - Credit Cards & Amazon Prime Fees – 120 (120) ( )
  - House Maintenance - 750 (740) ( )
  - Car Maintenance – 750 (700) (50,)
  - Medical Costs – 3,000 (2,850) (150,)

Total: $6,860.00 ($6,660.00)

Total Annual Recurring Expenses: $13,260.00 ($12,710.00)

SECTION 4

Annual Travel

Annual Total: - $3,600.00 ($3,600) ()

SECTION 5

Monthly Income

- **Bob's Monthly Paycheck: $2,500.00**
- **Janet's Monthly Paycheck: $3,333.00**

Total Take Home Pay: $5,833.00

SECTION 6

Savings And Investments

- **IRA – Bob - $62,000.00**
- **401K Plan - Janet - $88,000.00**
- **Joint Savings Account – $6,500.00**
- **TOTAL: $156,500.00**

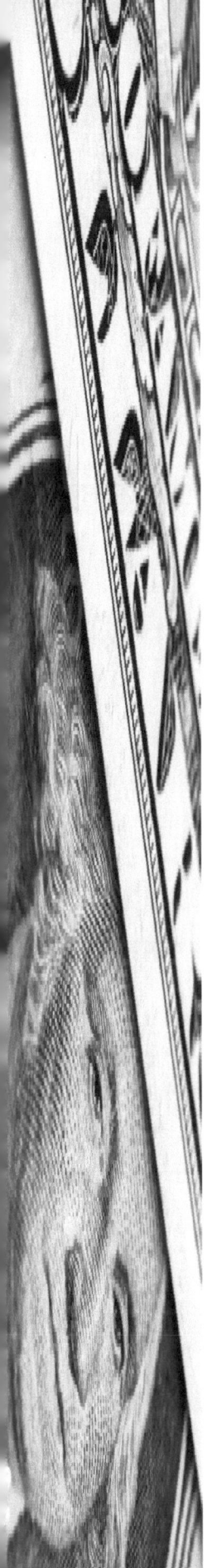
Janet takes each new charge and posts it on the appropriate line in the Dashboard, reducing the on-hand balance for that line based on the charge. For instance, she found a charge for $250 for groceries and she posted it on the Groceries budget line. Upon posting it, she subtracts that $250 from the $900 balance, creating a new balance of $650 (see Dashboard, Section 1).

Once Janet has completed all postings to the budget Dashboard lines, she will enter the new active credit balance for the open January Cycle (See JAN Cycle, Section 2).

The December Cycle credit card bill is scheduled for payment on the 10th of February (See Section 2) because that is when Janet scheduled it to be paid on-line. On the 10th of February, the December credit card balance will automatically be deducted from the joint checking account with auto-pay. Janet is confident that the required $900 balance is in the checking account because all the charges in December were debited from the Dashboard throughout the month and the funds to support them were not spent on other undocumented expenses.

"Never spend your money before you have earned it." – Thomas Jefferson

Annual Budget and Spending Plan
Monthly Budget for February 202_

This page built with Microsoft Power Point

SECTION 1
Monthly Budget - $5,833.00

- Bob's Allowance – 200 ( ) (, 25 Split dining out, 15 new wallet, 29 golf balls, 80 ATM,)
- Janet's Allowance – 200 (120) (15, 25 split, 6, 11, 23,)
- Mortgage – 700
- Auto Loan – 350
- Home & Auto Insurance – 300
- Emergency Fund – 300 (600) (300,)
- Electric – 80
- Natural Gas – 90
- Charity – 50 (40) (10,)
- Cell Phones –120
- Cable – 150
- Miscellaneous Expenses – 800 (751) (49 crock pot,)
- Groceries – 900 (650) (250,)
- Auto Gas – 188 (188)
- Annual Recurring Expenses – 1,105 (1,660) (755, 50 car service, 150 Med Supplement,)
- Travel = 300 (600) (300,)

TOTAL : $5,833.00 ($5,520.00)

SECTION 2
Current Credit Card Balances

- VISA (JAN Cycle) - $345.00 (Open)
- VISA (DEC Cycle) - $900.00.00 (Closed, Pay on 10 FEB)

SECTION 3
Annual Recurring Expenses

- Expenses Paid Quarterly
  - Water – 600 (450) (150,) (JAN, APR, JUL, OCT)
  - Home Association – 800 (600) (200,) (JAN, APR, JUL, OCT)

Total: $1,400.00 ($1,050.00)

- Expenses Paid Semi-Annually
  - House Tax – 2,500 (JUL/DEC)

Total: $5,000.00 ($5,000.00) If not paid with mortgage.

- Expenses Paid Annually:
  - Life Insurance Bob 800 (Due JUL)
  - Life Insurance Janet 650 (Due NOV)
  - Automobile Property Tax – 800 (800) (Due OCT)
  - Credit Cards & Amazon Prime Fees – 120 (120) ( )
  - House Maintenance - 750 (740) ( )
  - Car Maintenance – 750 (700) (50,)
  - Medical Costs – 3,000 (2,850) (150,)

Total: $6,860.00 ($6,660.00)

Total Annual Recurring Expenses: $13,260.00 ($12,710.00)

SECTION 4
Annual Travel

Annual Total: - $3,600.00 ($3,600) ()

SECTION 5
Monthly Income

- Bob's Monthly Paycheck: $2,500.00
- Janet's Monthly Paycheck: $3,333.00
- Total Take Home Pay: $5,833.00

SECTION 6
Savings And Investments

- IRA – Bob - $62,000.00
- 401K Plan - Janet - $88,000.00
- Joint Savings Account – $6,500.00
- TOTAL: $156,500.00

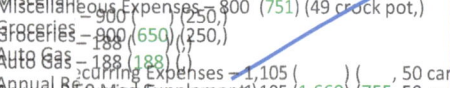

Section 3: Annual Recurring Expenses

1. Annual recurring expenses in most households are a big challenge: Time passes swiftly and these expenses sneak up on families and always seem to be an unwelcome surprise. The months when they come due are by no means fun and those who must pay them are sent scrambling to find a way to pay the bills on time. Section 3 of the Dashboard is set up so that not only does Janet know when those bills are due, the money is sitting there ready to go and she doesn't even give a second thought to paying them on time or even ahead of time if she will be away when they are due.

2. Bob and Janet have two bills which are paid quarterly. In January, Janet paid the water bill and home-owners association bills adjusting the balances of funds on hand for each. She then **bolded** and underlined JAN to indicate that these bills were paid. Then Janet adjusted the total quarterly balance on-hand from $1,400 to $1,050 and she also adjusted the Total Annual Recurring Expenses line at the bottom which now stands at $12,710 for the year.

3. Bob and Janet have one expense which is paid semi-annually, the house tax. The first payment is not due until July so nothing needs to be posted right now.

Annual Budget and Spending Plan
Monthly Budget for February 202_

This page built with Microsoft Power Point

SECTION 1

Monthly Budget - $5,833.00

- Bob's Allowance – 200 (61) (10, 25 Split dining out, 15 new wallet, 29 golf balls, 80 ATM,)
- Janet's Allowance – 200 (120) (15, 25 split, 6, 11, 23,)
- **Mortgage - 700**
- Auto Loan – 350
- Home & Auto Insurance – 300
- Emergency Fund – 300 (600) (300,)
- Electric – 80
- **Natural Gas – 90**
- Charity – 50 (40) (10,)
- Cell Phones –120
- **Cable – 150**
- Miscellaneous Expenses – 800 (751) (49 crock pot,)
- Groceries – 900 (650) (250,)
- Auto Gas – 188 (188) (,)
- Annual Recurring Expenses – 1,105 (1,660) (755, 50 car service, 150 Med Supplement,)
- **Travel – 300** (600) (300,)

TOTAL : $5,833.00 ($5,520.00)

SECTION 3

Annual Recurring Expenses

- **Expenses Paid Quarterly**
  - Water – 600 (450) (150,) (JAN, APR, JUL, OCT)
  - Home Association – 800 (600) (200,) (JAN, APR, JUL, OCT)

Total: $1,400.00 (1,050.00)

- **Expenses Paid Semi-Annually**
  - House Tax – 2,500 (JUL/DEC)

Total: $5,000.00 ($5,000.00) If not paid with mortgage.

- **Expenses Paid Annually:**
  - Life Insurance Bob 800 (Due JUL)
  - Life Insurance Janet 650 (Due NOV)
  - Automobile Property Tax – 800 (800) (Due OCT)
  - Credit Cards & Amazon Prime Fees – 120 (120) ( )
  - House Maintenance - 750 (740) ( )
  - Car Maintenance – 750 (700) (50,)
  - Medical Costs – 3,000 (2,850) (150,)

Total: $6,860.00 ($6,660.00)

Total Annual Recurring Expenses: $13,260.00 ($12,710.00)

SECTION 4

Annual Travel

Annual Total: - $3,600.00 ($3,600) ()

SECTION 5

Monthly Income

- Bob's Monthly Paycheck: $2,500.00
- Janet's Monthly Paycheck: $3,333.00

Total Take Home Pay: $5,833.00

SECTION 6

Savings And Investments

- IRA – Bob - $62,000.00
- 401K Plan - Janet - $88,000.00
- Joint Savings Account – $6,500.00
- TOTAL: $156,500.00

SECTION 2

Current Credit Card Balances

- VISA (JAN Cycle) - $345.00 (Open)
- VISA (DEC Cycle) – $900.00.00 (Closed, Pay on 10 FEB)

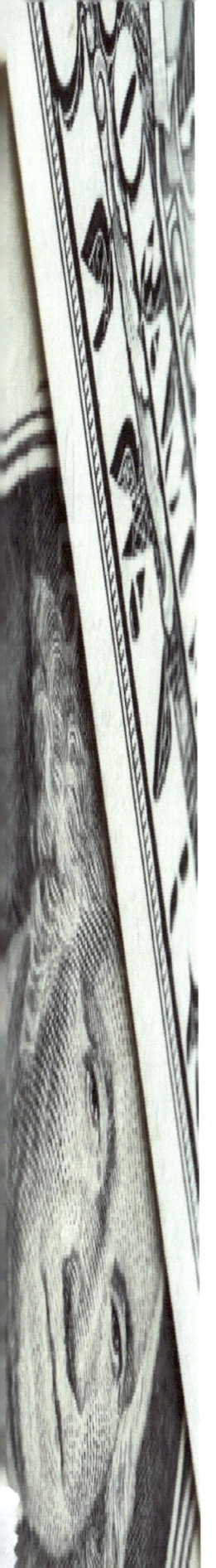

④ Bob and Janet have seven recurring annual expense lines which are paid annually or throughout the year. Not all of these are paid as a single payment like life insurance. Some categories, like Car Maintenance and Medical Costs are a budget estimate of what they expect they will need for a particular kind of expense throughout the year. Bob and Janet have created these expense categories in order to protect their monthly budget from the turbulence which might be caused from a plumbers visit, a car repair or a medical expense. So far this year, Bob spent $50 to get an oil and filter change on his car and Janet paid $150 for prescription drugs. In each case, Janet adjusted the remaining balance on each of these lines, adjusted the balance on the Annual Expense Total to $6,660, and then adjusted the balance remaining on the Total Annual Recurring Expenses line at the bottom which now stands at $12,710 for the year.

⑤ It is very important to keep the Dashboard in balance and to check your work. If this is not done, the Dashboard will become error filled. When Janet wants to do a quick audit of Section 3, she will add up the balances remaining (green figures) for Quarterly, Semi-annual, and Annual Expenses and make certain that they add up to the green remaining balance for Total Annual Recurring Expenses.

35

Annual Budget and Spending Plan
Monthly Budget for February 202_

This page built with Microsoft Power Point

SECTION 1
Monthly Budget - $5,833.00

- Bob's Allowance – 200 ( ) (, 25 Split dining out, 15 new wallet; 29 golf balls, 80 ATM,)
- Janet's Allowance – 200 (120) (15, 25 split, 6, 11, 23,)
- Mortgage – 700
- Auto Loan – 350
- Home & Auto Insurance – 300
- Emergency Fund – 300 (600) (300,)
- Electric – 80
- Natural Gas – 90
- Charity – 50 (40) (10,)
- Cell Phones – 120
- Cable – 150
- Miscellaneous Expenses – 800 (751) (49 crock pot,)
- Groceries – 900 (650) (250,)
- Auto Gas – 188 (188) ( )
- Annual Recurring Expenses – 1,105 (1,660) (755, 50 car service, 150 Med Supplement,)
- Travel – 300 (600) (300,)

TOTAL : $5,833.00 ($5,520.00)

SECTION 2
Current Credit Card Balances

- VISA (JAN Cycle) - $345.00 (Open)
- VISA (DEC Cycle) – $900.00.00 (Closed, Pay on 10 FEB)

SECTION 3
Annual Recurring Expenses

- Expenses Paid Quarterly
  - Water – 600 (450) (150,) JAN, APR, JUL, OCT
  - Home Association – 800 (600) (200,) JAN, APR, JUL, OCT

Total: $1,400.00 (1,050.00)

- Expenses Paid Semi-Annually
  - House Tax – 2,500 (JUL/DEC)

Total: $5,000.00 ($5,000.00) If not paid with mortgage.

- Expenses Paid Annually:
  - Life Insurance Bob 800 (Due JUL)
  - Life Insurance Janet 650 (Due NOV)
  - Automobile Property Tax – 800 (800) (Due OCT)
  - Credit Cards & Amazon Prime Fees – 120 (120) ( )
  - House Maintenance – 750 (740) ( )
  - Car Maintenance – 750 (700) (50,)
  - Medical Costs – 3,000 (2,850) (150,)

Total: $6,860.00 ($6,660.00)

Total Annual Recurring Expenses: $13,260.00 ($12,710.00)

SECTION 4
Annual Travel

Annual Total: - $3,600.00 ($3,600) ()

SECTION 5
Monthly Income

- Bob's Monthly Paycheck: $2,500.00
- Janet's Monthly Paycheck: $3,333.00

Total Take Home Pay: $5,833.00

SECTION 6
Savings And Investments

- IRA – Bob - $62,000.00
- 401K Plan - Janet - $88,000.00
- Joint Savings Account – $6,500.00
- TOTAL: $156,500.00

Once she obtains that figure, she will go to the Annual Recurring Expenses line in Section 1. There, she will multiply the monthly budgeted figure in black ($1,105) times the number of months remaining in the year (10). This will give her the projected accumulation of funds ($11,050) for the remaining ten months. Next, Alice will add the $11,050 to the current balance in February of $1,660 which will give her a balance of $12,710 which is the same balance at the bottom of Section 3. The Dashboard is now balanced and on track with respect to Annual Recurring Expenses.

At this point, it is important to note a key difference between the green on-hand balances in Section 1 and the green balances in Sections 3 and 4. In Section 1, a green balance denotes that actual cash is on-hand in the joint checking account to cover this balance. However, in Section 3, the green balances are fed directly to it from the Annual Recurring Expenses line in Section 1. It important to understand that everything which happens in Section 3 is based on the monthly accumulating balance on the Annual Recurring Expense line in Section 1. In other words, Section 3 has no cash assets of its own so the monthly budget must feed and sustain everything in Section 3 throughout the year.

Annual Budget and Spending Plan
Monthly Budget for February 202_

This page built with Microsoft Power Point

SECTION 1

Monthly Budget - $5,833.00

- Bob's Allowance – 200 (61) (10, 25 Split dining out, 15 new wallet, 29 golf balls, 80 ATM,)
- Janet's Allowance – 200 (120) (15, 25 split, 6, 11, 23,)
- **Mortgage - 700**
- Auto Loan – 350
- Home & Auto Insurance – 300
- Emergency Fund – 300 (600) (300,)
- Electric – 80
- **Natural Gas – 90**
- Charity – 50 (40) (10,)
- Cell Phones –120
- **Cable – 150**
- Miscellaneous Expenses – 800 (751) (49 crock pot,)
- Groceries – 900 (650) (250,)
- Auto Gas – 188 (188) (,)
- Annual Recurring Expenses – 1,105 (1,660) (755, 50 car service, 150 Med Supplement,)
- **Travel – 300** (600) (300,)

TOTAL : $5,833.00 ($5,520.00)

SECTION 3

① Annual Recurring Expenses

- **Expenses Paid Quarterly**
    - Water – 600 (450) (150,) (JAN, APR, JUL, OCT)
    - Home Association – 800 (600) (200,) (JAN, APR, JUL, OCT)

Total: $1,400.00 (1,050.00)

- **Expenses Paid Semi-Annually**
    - House Tax – 2,500 (JUL/DEC)

Total: $5,000.00 ($5,000.00) If not paid with mortgage.

- **Expenses Paid Annually:**
    - Life Insurance Bob 800 (Due JUL)
    - Life Insurance Janet 650 (Due NOV)
    - Automobile Property Tax – 800 (800) (Due OCT)
    - Credit Cards & Amazon Prime Fees – 120 (120) ( )
    - House Maintenance - 750 (740) ( )
    - Car Maintenance – 750 (700) (50,)
    - Medical Costs – 3,000 (2,850) (150,)

Total: $6,860.00 ($6,660.00)

Total Annual Recurring Expenses: $13,260.00 ($12,710.00)

SECTION 4

Annual Travel

Annual Total: - $3,600.00 ($3,600) ()

SECTION 5

Monthly Income

- Bob's Monthly Paycheck: $2,500.00
- Janet's Monthly Paycheck: $3,333.00

Total Take Home Pay: $5,833.00

SECTION 6

Savings And Investments

- IRA – Bob - $62,000.00
- 401K Plan - Janet - $88,000.00
- Joint Savings Account – $6,500.00
- **TOTAL: $156,500.00**

SECTION 2

Current Credit Card Balances

- VISA (JAN Cycle) - $345.00 (Open)
- VISA (DEC Cycle) – $900.00.00 (Closed, Pay on 10 FEB)

The same process applies to Travel. In Section 4, the green balance is fed directly from the Travel line in Section 1. It is important to understand that everything which happens in Section 4 is based on the monthly accumulating balance on the Travel line in Section 1. In other words, Section 4 has no cash assets of its own so the monthly budget must feed and sustain Section 4.

Another way to remember all of this is that Section 1, the Monthly Budget, has dedicated funds from the joint checking account whereas Sections 3 and 4 have only allocated funds from Section 1 which accumulate monthly.

"Money is a terrible master but an excellent servant." – P.T. Barnum

Annual Budget and Spending Plan
Monthly Budget for February 202_

This page built with Microsoft Power Point

SECTION 1
Monthly Budget - $5,833.00

- Bob's Allowance – 200 ( ) ( ) 25 Split dining out, 15 new wallet, 29 golf balls, 80 ATM
- Janet's Allowance – 200 (120) (15, 25 split, 6, 11, 23,)
- Mortgage – 700
- Auto Loan – 350
- Home & Auto Insurance – 300
- Emergency Fund – 300 (600) (300,)
- Electric – 80
- Natural Gas – 90
- Charity – 50 (40) (10,)
- Cell Phones – 120
- Cable – 150
- Miscellaneous Expenses – 800 (751) (49 crock pot,)
- Groceries – 900 (650) (250,)
- Auto Gas – 188 (188)
- Annual Recurring Expenses – 1,105 (1,660) (755, 50 car service, 150 Med Supplement,)
- Travel = 300 (600) (300,)

TOTAL : $5,833.00 ($5,520.00)

SECTION 2
Current Credit Card Balances

- **VISA (JAN Cycle) - $345.00 (Open)**
- VISA (DEC Cycle) – $900.00.00 (Closed, Pay on 10 FEB)

SECTION 3
Annual Recurring Expenses

- Expenses Paid Quarterly
  - Water – 600 (450) (150,) (JAN, APR, JUL, OCT)
  - Home Association – 800 (600) (200,) (JAN, APR, JUL, OCT)

Total: $1,400.00 (1,050.00)

- Expenses Paid Semi-Annually
  - House Tax – 2,500 (JUL/DEC)

Total: $5,000.00 ($5,000.00)

- Expenses Paid Annually:
  - Life Insurance Bob 800 (Due JUL)
  - Life Insurance Janet 650 (Due NOV)
  - Automobile Property Tax – 800 (Due OCT)
  - Credit Cards & Amazon Prime Fees – 120 (120) ( )
  - House Maintenance – 750 (740) ( )
  - Car Maintenance – 750 (700) (50,)
  - Medical Costs – 3,000 (2,850) (150,)

Total: $6,860.00 ($6,660.00)

Total Annual Recurring Expenses: $13,260.00 ($12,710.00)

SECTION 4
Annual Travel

Annual Total: - $3,600.00 ($3,600) ()

SECTION 5
Monthly Income

- Bob's Monthly Paycheck: $2,500.00
- Janet's Monthly Paycheck: $3,333.00

Total Take Home Pay: $5,833.00

Savings And Investments

- IRA – Bob - $62,000.00
- 401K Plan - Janet - $88,000.00
- Joint Savings Account – $6,500.00
- **TOTAL: $156,500.00**

Section 4: Annual Travel

1. Both Bob and Janet work hard but try to take a couple of vacations each year. Their favorite thing to do is visit different national parks and go backpacking on trails with some of the most beautiful scenery in the world. Their enjoyment of these trips is their reason for saving something for travel from every paycheck.

2. Bob and Janet have decided to allocate $3,600 per year to fund their two vacations. They start by having a monthly budget line for Travel in Section 1 of the Dashboard. They have allocated $300 per month to this line which after two months in this budget year has accrued to $600, which is also present in the checking account. The second set of parentheses on the Section 1 Travel line shows that $300 was brought forward from January. Every month, another $300 will be added to the Travel line in Section 1 and will by December become the $3,600 allocated for annual travel in Section 4. Bob and Alice usually try to take one vacation in June when they have $1,800 saved on the Dashboard and in checking, and another vacation in October after another $1,200 has accrued on the Dashboard and in checking. They tend to switch between air travel and road travel so that they never use more than they have saved for Travel. Since they run most of their budget through an air miles generating credit card, they use these miles to reduce their air travel costs.

Annual Budget and Spending Plan
Monthly Budget for February 202_

This page built with Microsoft Power Point

SECTION 1

Monthly Budget - $5,833.00

- Bob's Allowance – 200 (61) (10, 25 Split dining out, 15 new wallet, 29 golf balls, 80 ATM,)
- Janet's Allowance – 200 (120) (15, 25 split, 6, 11, 23,)
- **Mortgage - 700**
- Auto Loan – 350
- Home & Auto Insurance – 300
- Emergency Fund – 300 (600) (300,)
- Electric – 80
- **Natural Gas – 90**
- Charity – 50 (40) (10,)
- Cell Phones –120
- **Cable – 150**
- Miscellaneous Expenses – 800 (751) (49 crock pot,)
- Groceries – 900 (650) (250,)
- Auto Gas – 188 (188) (,)
- Annual Recurring Expenses – 1,105 (1,660) (755, 50 car service, 150 Med Supplement,)
- **Travel – 300** (600) (300,)

TOTAL : $5,833.00 ($5,520.00)

SECTION 3

Annual Recurring Expenses

- **Expenses Paid Quarterly**
  - Water – 600 (450) (150,) (JAN, APR, JUL, OCT)
  - Home Association – 800 (600) (200,) (JAN, APR, JUL, OCT)

Total: $1,400.00 (1,050.00)

- **Expenses Paid Semi-Annually**
  - House Tax – 2,500 (JUL/DEC)

Total: $5,000.00 ($5,000.00)

- **Expenses Paid Annually:**
  - Life Insurance Bob 800 (Due JUL)
  - Life Insurance Janet 650 (Due NOV)
  - Automobile Property Tax – 800 (Due OCT)
  - Credit Cards & Amazon Prime Fees – 120 (120) ( )
  - House Maintenance - 750 (740) ( )
  - Car Maintenance – 750 (700) (50,)
  - Medical Costs – 3,000 (2,850) (150,)

Total: $6,860.00 ($6,660.00)

Total Annual Recurring Expenses: $13,260.00 ($12,710.00)

SECTION 4

Annual Travel

Annual Total: - $3,600.00 ($3,600) ()

SECTION 5

Monthly Income

- Bob's Monthly Paycheck: $2,500.00
- Janet's Monthly Paycheck: $3,333.00

Total Take Home Pay: $5,833.00

SECTION 2

Current Credit Card Balances

- VISA (JAN Cycle) - $345.00 (Open)
- VISA (DEC Cycle) – $900.00.00 (Closed, Pay on 10 FEB)

SECTION 6

Savings And Investments

- IRA – Bob - $62,000.00
- 401K Plan - Janet - $88,000.00
- Joint Savings Account – $6,500.00
- **TOTAL: $156,500.00**

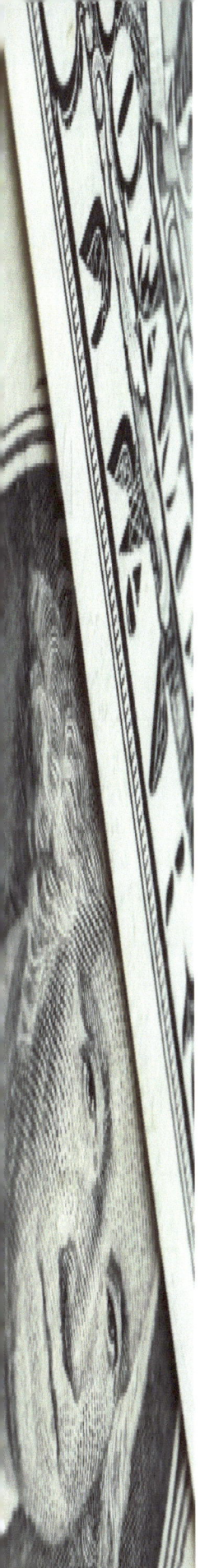

Section 5: Monthly Income

In our example, Total Take Home Pay in Section 5 is the starting point for populating the Dashboard. Total Take Home Pay is the planning basis for the Monthly Budget whereas total Take Home Pay X 12 is the planning basis for the Annual Budget and Spending Plan. Other sources of funds could have been used instead of Total Take Home Pay. Some people maintain two checkbooks, one for their budgeted recurring expenses and another for everything else. In this way, some funds are reserved for the "no fail" bills in the Dashboard while the rest are available for discretionary spending outside the Dashboard.

At the bottom of Section 1 there are two numbers. The number in black represents the full budget for February and matches both the number in the Section 1 heading and the Total Take Home Pay figure in Section 5. The number in green at the bottom of Section 1 ($5,520) is very important because that number represents a current snapshot of the amount of funds remaining in the Dashboard monthly budget (Section 1) after all expenditures paid by check or credit card have been posted to the budget lines.

Based on what we know about Sections 1 thru 5, let's do a quick audit to see if Bob and Janet are on track. The total funds still available for all budget

Annual Budget and Spending Plan
Monthly Budget for February 202_

This page built with Microsoft Power Point

SECTION 1
Monthly Budget - $5,833.00

- Bob's Allowance – 200 (ATM, 25 Split dining out, 15 new wallet, 29 golf balls, 80 ATM,)
- Janet's Allowance – 200 (120) (15, 25 split, 6, 11, 23,)
- Mortgage – 700
- Auto Loan – 350
- Home & Auto Insurance – 300
- Emergency Fund – 300 (600) (300,)
- Electric – 80
- Natural Gas – 90 (10,)
- Charity – 50 (49) (10,)
- Cell Phones – 120
- Cable – 150
- Miscellaneous Expenses – 800 (751) (49 crock pot,)
- Groceries – 900 (650) (250,)
- Auto Gas – 188 (188)
- Annual Recurring Expenses – 1,105 (1,660) (755, 50 car service, 150 Med Supplement,)
- Travel – 300 (600) (300,)

TOTAL : $5,833.00 ($5,520.00)

SECTION 2
Current Credit Card Balances

- VISA (JAN Cycle) - $345.00 (Open)
- VISA (DEC Cycle) – $900.00.00 (Closed, Pay on 10 FEB)

SECTION 3
Annual Recurring Expenses

- Expenses Paid Quarterly
  - Water – 600 (450) (150,) (JAN, APR, JUL, OCT)
  - Home Association – 800 (600) (200,) (JAN, APR, JUL, OCT)

Total: $1,400.00 (1,050.00)

- Expenses Paid Semi-Annually
  - House Tax – 2,500 (JUL/DEC)

Total: $5,000.00 ($5,000.00)

- Expenses Paid Annually:
  - Life Insurance Bob 800 (Due JUL)
  - Life Insurance Janet 650 (Due NOV)
  - Automobile Property Tax – 800 (Due OCT)
  - Credit Cards & Amazon Prime Fees – 120 (120) ( )
  - House Maintenance – 750 (740) ( )
  - Car Maintenance – 750 (700) (50,)
  - Medical Costs – 3,000 (2,850) (150,)

Total: $6,860.00 ($6,660.00)

Total Annual Recurring Expenses: $13,260.00 ($12,710.00)

SECTION 4
Annual Travel

Annual Total: - $3,600.00 ($3,600) ()

SECTION 5
Monthly Income

- Bob's Monthly Paycheck: $2,500.00
- Janet's Monthly Paycheck: $3,333.00

Total Take Home Pay: $5,833.00

SECTION 6
Savings And Investments

- IRA – Bob - $62,000.00
- 401K Plan - Janet - $88,000.00
- Joint Savings Account – $6,500.00
- **TOTAL: $156,500.00**

lines is derived by adding up the green balances in the first parentheses plus the single bill non-bolded budget lines in Section 1. These add up to $5,520 which matches the $5.520 in green on the TOTAL line. Now add that $5,520 to the Open Visa balance of $345 and the Closed Visa balance of $900 and you have a grand total of $6,765. If you were to go to Bob and Janet's joint check book, that checkbook balance should be exactly $6,765. Maybe you noticed that $6,765 is more than the monthly budget of $5,833. This is because funds to cover both the open and closed credit card balances are still in the check book from charges made from mid DEC through today and subtracted from Section 1 line balances. If the combined balances of for Sections 1 and 2 on the Dashboard of $6,765 are not in the checking account, then it is time for Janet to review all transactions to try and figure out where the accounting error is. Much of the time it is simply due to not updating the Dashboard with all current checks and charges before doing the audit. Don't worry, like any new system, the longer you maintain the Dashboard, the more routine and accurate it will become. Once you are familiar with your budget dashboard system, you should spend no more than four ten-minute sessions per week to maintain an accurate financial picture down to the dollar.

Annual Budget and Spending Plan
Monthly Budget for February 202_

This page built with Microsoft Power Point

SECTION 1

Monthly Budget - $5,833.00

- Bob's Allowance – 200 (61) (10, 25 Split dining out, 15 new wallet, 29 golf balls, 80 ATM,)
- Janet's Allowance – 200 (120) (15, 25 split, 6, 11, 23,)
- **Mortgage - 700**
- Auto Loan – 350
- Home & Auto Insurance – 300
- Emergency Fund – 300 (600) (300,)
- Electric – 80
- **Natural Gas – 90**
- Charity – 50 (40) (10,)
- Cell Phones –120
- **Cable – 150**
- Miscellaneous Expenses – 800 (751) (49 crock pot,)
- Groceries – 900 (650) (250,)
- Auto Gas – 188 (188) (,)
- Annual Recurring Expenses – 1,105 (1,660) (755, 50 car service, 150 Med Supplement,)
- **Travel – 300** (600) (300,)

TOTAL : $5,833.00 ($5,520.00)

SECTION 2

Current Credit Card Balances

- VISA (JAN Cycle) - $345.00 (Open)
- VISA (DEC Cycle) – $900.00.00 (Closed, Pay on 10 FEB)

SECTION 3

Annual Recurring Expenses

- **Expenses Paid Quarterly**
  - Water – 600 (450) (150,) (JAN, APR, JUL, OCT)
  - Home Association – 800 (600) (200,) (JAN, APR, JUL, OCT)

Total: $1,400.00 (1,050.00)

- **Expenses Paid Semi-Annually**
  - House Tax – 2,500 (JUL/DEC)

Total: $5,000.00 ($5,000.00)

Expenses Paid Annually:
  - Life Insurance Bob 800 (Due JUL)
  - Life Insurance Janet 650 (Due NOV)
  - Automobile Property Tax – 800 (Due OCT)
  - Credit Cards & Amazon Prime Fees – 120 (120) ( )
  - House Maintenance - 750 (740) ( )
  - Car Maintenance – 750 (700) (50,)
  - Medical Costs – 3,000 (2,850) (150,)

Total: $6,860.00 ($6,660.00)

Total Annual Recurring Expenses: $13,260.00 ($12,710.00)

SECTION 4

Annual Travel

Annual Total: - $3,600.00 ($3,600) ()

SECTION 5

Monthly Income

- **Bob's Monthly Paycheck: $2,500.00**
- **Janet's Monthly Paycheck: $3,333.00**

Total Take Home Pay: $5,833.00

SECTION 6

Savings And Investments

- IRA – Bob - $62,000.00 (1 JAN 21)
- 401K Plan - Janet - $88,000.00 (1 JAN 21)
- Joint Savings Account – $6,500.00 (1 JAN 21)

TOTAL: $156,500.00

Section 6:
Savings and Investments

The Dashboard is a great place to keep track of savings and investment balances like Bob and Janet have done. They update this area every six months, even placing the date behind each balance as a time reference. This is an area where one can also be very creative.

Some older savers are focused on retirement so they enter such things as projected monthly Social Security income, projected work retirement plan income, and income from an annuity which they might purchase with their IRA/401K plan. Then they total these up to watch their future retirement incomes grow during each periodic checkup.

People with children might list the balances of each child's current education savings plan balance. All these entries can add up to provide a sense of future financial security or a red flag that the savings rate is not yet where it needs to be. Just seeing what you have accrued in one place every time you view the Dashboard is a great financial status feedback mechanism.

"Money can't buy you happiness, but it helps you look for it in a lot more places." - Milton Berle

Annual Budget and Spending Plan
Monthly Budget for December 202_

This page built with Microsoft Power Point

SECTION 1

Monthly Budget - $5,833.00

- Bob's Allowance – 200 ( ) (5) (50, 55 flowers, 40 eat out, 50 eat out,)
- Janet's Allowance – 200 (19) (80, 25, 16, 22, 1, 85, 19, 33, 60,)
- Mortgage – 700
- Auto Loan – 350
- Home & Auto Insurance – 300
- Emergency Fund – 300 (2,100) (1,800,)
- Electric – 80 – 90
- Natural Gas – 90
- Charity – 50 (10, 10, 10, 10,)
- Cell Phone – 120
- Cable – 150
- Miscellaneous Expenses – 800 (13) (49, 40, 140, 95, 23, 13, 11, 40, 56, 32, 90, 102, 120, 175, 125, 100,)
- Groceries – 900 (150, 50, 200, 275, 25, 100,)
- Auto Gas – 188 (38) (25, 40, 30, 25, 30,)
- Annual Recurring Expenses – 1,105 (3,350) (3045, 800 Bob dental work,)
- Travel = 300 (100) (400,)

TOTAL: $5,833.00 ($5,559.00)

SECTION 2

Current Credit Card Balances

- VISA (NOV/DEC Billing Cycle) - $1,574.00 (Open)
- VISA (DEC/JAN Billing Cycle) – $0.00.00 (Pending)

SECTION 3

Annual Recurring Expenses

- Expenses Paid Quarterly
  - Water – 600 (0) (150, 150, 150, 150) (JAN, APR, JUL, OCT)
  - Home Association – 800 (0) (200, 200, 200, 200) (JAN, APR, JUL, OCT)

Total: $1,400.00 (0.00)

- Expenses Paid Semi-Annually
  - House Tax – 2,500 (JUL/DEC)

Total: $5,000.00 ($2,500.00)

- Expenses Paid Annually:
  - Life Insurance Bob - 800 (Due JUL)
  - Life Insurance Janet – 750 (D) (Due NOV)
  - Automobile & Boat Tax – 800 (Due OCT)
  - Credit Cards & Amazon Prime Fees – 120 (0) (90, 30)
  - House Maintenance – 750 (240) (300, 150, 50,)
  - Car Maintenance – 1,000 (210) (50, 250, 100, 90)
  - Medical Costs – 3,000 (400) (150, 1,500, 800,)

Total: $6,860.00 ($850.00)

Total Annual Recurring Expenses: $13,260.00 ($3,350.00)

SECTION 4

Annual Travel

Annual Total: - $3,600.00 ($100.00) ()

SECTION 5

Monthly Income

- Bob's Monthly Paycheck: $2,500.00
- Janet's Monthly Paycheck: $3,333.00

Total Take Home Pay: $5,833.00

SECTION 6

Savings And Investments

- IRA – Bob - $62,000.00
- 401K Plan - Janet - $88,000.00
- Joint Savings Account – $6,500.00

TOTAL: $156,500.00

The December Budget

In our example, we have jumped ahead to December, about a week before Christmas, to see how Bob and Janet's now "mature" annual budget has fared over the past year and during this last month of the year. Let's look at their budget Dashboard.

In Section 1, it appears that most of the monthly bills have been paid because they have been **bolded**.

The balances in Bob's and Janet's allowances are down to $5 and $19 respectively for the month and this could be a problem because they are just now purchasing Christmas gifts for one another using the credit card.

The Emergency Fund is healthy with a balance of $2,100 after $1,800 was brought forward from November. The Emergency fund could have achieved its annual maximum of $3,600 if not for a week-long emergency visit Janet made to see her mother who had health issues. This trip required $1,500 to be taken from the Emergency Fund. Fortunately, this trip could be undertaken with no disruption to either the monthly budget or the annual spending plan. Janet and Bob are excited about carrying over the remaining $2,100 Emergency Fund balance to the next budget year.

Annual Budget and Spending Plan
Monthly Budget for December 202_

This page built with Microsoft Power Point

SECTION 1

Monthly Budget - $5,833.00

- Bob's Allowance – 200 (5) (50, 55 flowers, 40 eat out, 50 eat out,)
- Janet's Allowance – 200 (19) (80, 25, 16, 22, 1, 85, 19, 33, 60,)
- **Mortgage - 700**
- **Auto Loan – 350**
- **Home & Auto Insurance – 300**
- Emergency Fund – 300 (2,100) (1,800,)
- **Electric – 80**
- **Natural Gas – 90**
- Charity – 50 (10) (10, 10, 10, 10,)
- **Cell Phones –120**
- **Cable – 150**
- Miscellaneous Expenses – 800 (13) (49, 40, 140, 95, 23, 15, 11, 40, 56, 32, 90, 102, 120,)
- Groceries – 900 (150) (150, 200, 175, 125, 100,)
- Auto Gas – 188 (38) (25, 40, 30, 25, 30,)
- Annual Recurring Expenses – 1,105 (3,350) (3045, 800 Bob dental work,)
- Travel – 300 (100) (400,)

TOTAL : $5,833.00 ($5,559.00)

SECTION 2

Current Credit Card Balances

- VISA (NOV/DEC Billing Cycle) - $1,574.00 (Open)
- VISA (DEC/JAN Billing Cycle) – $0.00.00 (Pending)

SECTION 3

Annual Recurring Expenses

- **Expenses Paid Quarterly**
  - **Water – 600** (0) (150, 150, 150, 150) (JAN, APR, JUL, OCT)
  - **Home Association** – 800 (0) (200, 200, 200, 200) (JAN, APR, JUL, OCT)

Total: $1,400.00 (0.00)

- **Expenses Paid Semi-Annually**
  - House Tax – 2,500 (JUL/DEC)

Total: $5,000.00 ($2,500.00)

- **Expenses Paid Annually:**
  - Life Insurance Bob - 800 (Due JUL)
  - Life Insurance Janet - 650 (Due NOV)
  - Automobile Property Tax – 800 (Due OCT)
  - Credit Cards & Amazon Prime Fees – 120 (0) (90, 30)
  - House Maintenance - 750 (240) (300, 150, 50,)
  - Car Maintenance – 750 (210) (50, 250, 100, 90)
  - Medical Costs – 3,000 (400) (150, 1,500, 800,)

Total: $6,860.00 ($850.00)

Total Annual Recurring Expenses: $13,260.00 ($3,350.00)

SECTION 4

Annual Travel

Annual Total: - $3,600.00 ($100.00) ()

SECTION 5

Monthly Income

- **Bob's Monthly Paycheck: $2,500.00**
- **Janet's Monthly Paycheck: $3,333.00**

Total Take Home Pay: $5,833.00

SECTION 6

Savings And Investments

- IRA – Bob - $62,000.00
- 401K Plan - Janet - $88,000.00
- Joint Savings Account – $6,500.00

TOTAL: $156,500.00

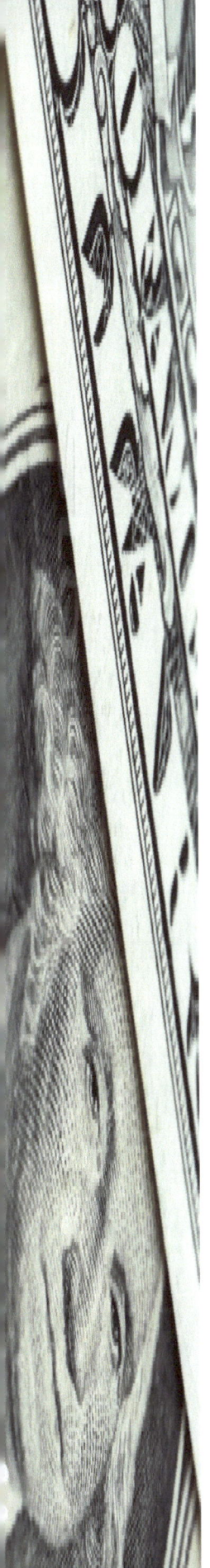

We see that Miscellaneous Expenses are currently in the red by $13 while Groceries and Auto Gas are in the green by $150 and $38 respectively.

The Annual Recurring Expenses line has a balance of $3,350 after a balance of $3,045 was brought forward from November and after Bob wrote a check to his dentist for $800 dollars.

The Travel line is in the red $100 as Bob and Janet approach both the end of the month and the end of the year.

Finally, there is a Section 1 Total on-hand balance of $5,559 which is also sitting in the joint checking account ready to finish out the year.

Alice is thinking that she may soon be able to cross-level the surplus funds for groceries and gas to make up for the miscellaneous and travel deficits. She also has her eye on some available funds in Section 3 which she and Bob have agreed can be used to offset Christmas gift expenses. It looks like things are working out well financially here at the end of the year.

In Section 2, the open November/December billing cycle balance on the the VISA credit card account now stands at $1,574 but it will close tomorrow for payment in January. That will then begin the December/January billing cycle. The $1,574 dollars reflected in Section 2 are on hand in and covered by the joint checking account just as are the $5,559 dollars in Section 1.

Annual Budget and Spending Plan
Monthly Budget for December 202_

This page built with Microsoft Power Point

SECTION 1

Monthly Budget - $5,833.00

- Bob's Allowance – 200 (5) (50, 55 flowers, 40 eat out, 50 eat out;)
- Janet's Allowance – 200 (19) (80, 25, 16, 22, 1, 85, 19, 33, 60;)
- Mortgage – 700
- Auto Loan – 350
- Home & Auto Insurance – 300
- Emergency Fund – 300 (2,100) (1,800,)
- Electric – 80
- Natural Gas – 90
- Charity – 50 (10) (10, 10, 10, 10,)
- Cell Phones – 120
- Cable – 150
- Miscellaneous Expenses – 800 (13) (49, 40, 140, 95, 23, 15, 11, 40, 56, 32, 90, 102, 120,)
- Groceries – 900 (150) (150, 200, 175, 125, 100,)
- Auto Gas – 188 (38) (25, 40, 30, 25, 30,)
- Annual Recurring Expenses – 1,105 (3,350) (3045, 800 Bob dental work,) ( )
- Travel – 300 (100) (400,)

TOTAL : $5,833.00 ($5,559.00)

SECTION 2

Current Credit Card Balances

- VISA (NOV/DEC Billing Cycle) - $1,574.00 (Open)
- VISA (DEC/JAN Billing Cycle) – $0.00.00 (Pending)

SECTION 3

Annual Recurring Expenses

- Expenses Paid Quarterly
  - Water – 600 (0) (150, 150, 150, 150) (JAN, APR, JUL, OCT)
  - Home Association – 800 (0) (200, 200, 200, 200) (JAN, APR, JUL, OCT)

Total: $1,400.00 (0.00)

- Expenses Paid Semi-Annually
  - House Tax – 2,500 (JUL/DEC)

Total: $5,000.00 ($2,500.00)

- Expenses Paid Annually:
  - Life Insurance Bob - 800 (Due JUL)
  - Life Insurance Janet - 650 (Due NOV)
  - Automobile Property Tax – 800 (Due OCT)
  - Credit Cards & Amazon Prime Fees – 120 (0) (90, 30)
  - House Maintenance – 750 (240) (300, 150, 50,)
  - Car Maintenance – 3,000 (210) (150, 250, 100, 90)
  - Medical Costs – 3,000 (400) (150, 1,500, 800,)

Total: $6,860.00 ($850.00)

Total Annual Recurring Expenses: $13,260.00 ($3,350.00)

SECTION 4

Annual Travel

Annual Total: - $3,600.00 ($100.00) ()

SECTION 5

Monthly Income

- Bob's Monthly Paycheck: $2,500.00
- Janet's Monthly Paycheck: $3,333.00

Total Take Home Pay: $5,833.00

SECTION 6

Savings And Investments

- IRA – Bob - $62,000.00
- 401K Plan - Janet - $88,000.00
- Joint Savings Account – $6,500.00

TOTAL: $156,500.00

Remember, the Dashboard and its supporting checking account are linked, mutually supporting financial instruments. There should always be an exact match between the checking account balance and the total balance in Section 1, plus the open/closed credit card balances in Section 2.

Section 3 is maintaining a healthy glidepath as the year comes to an end. Both quarterly expense lines for Water and Home Association have been paid and are now at zero balance for the year. The words Water and Home Association have been **bolded** to indicate that those lines are now completed and closed. Each of the months when quarterly payments were made were **bolded** and <u>underlined</u> at the time they were paid. These visual signals (bolding and underlining) help save time when performing periodic audits on the Dashboard because they let one move quickly through that section. The Total funds available for Quarterly Recurring Expenses is now (0).

Expenses Paid Semi-Annually has a current on-hand balance of ($2,500) but the December house tax payment is due this week which will close this line out for the year.

Four of the seven lines under Expenses Paid Annually are now at 0 balance but three areas have funds left which are available for use in other areas. These are the funds which Bob and Janet have agreed to tap into to augment their allowances to

Annual Budget and Spending Plan
Monthly Budget for December 202_

This page built with Microsoft Power Point

SECTION 1

Monthly Budget - $5,833.00

- Bob's Allowance – 200 (5) (50, 55 flowers, 40 eat out, 50 eat out,)
- Janet's Allowance – 200 (19) (80, 25, 16, 22, 1, 85, 19, 33, 60,)
- **Mortgage - 700**
- **Auto Loan – 350**
- **Home & Auto Insurance – 300**
- Emergency Fund – 300 (2,100) (1,800,)
- **Electric – 80**
- **Natural Gas – 90**
- Charity – 50 (10) (10, 10, 10, 10,)
- **Cell Phones –120**
- **Cable – 150**
- Miscellaneous Expenses – 800 (13) (49, 40, 140, 95, 23, 15, 11, 40, 56, 32, 90, 102, 120,)
- Groceries – 900 (150) (150, 200, 175, 125, 100,)
- Auto Gas – 188 (38) (25, 40, 30, 25, 30,)
- Annual Recurring Expenses – 1,105 (3,350) (3045, 800 Bob dental work,)
- Travel – 300 (100) (400,)

TOTAL : $5,833.00 ($5,559.00)

SECTION 2
Current Credit Card Balances

- VISA (NOV/DEC Billing Cycle) - $1,574.00 (Open)
- VISA (DEC/JAN Billing Cycle) – $0.00.00 (Pending)

SECTION 3

Annual Recurring Expenses

- **Expenses Paid Quarterly**
  - **Water – 600** (0) (150, 150, 150, 150) (JAN, APR, JUL, OCT)
  - **Home Association – 800** (0) (200, 200, 200, 200) (JAN, APR, JUL, OCT)

Total: **$1,400.00** (0.00)

- **Expenses Paid Semi-Annually**
  - House Tax – 2,500 (JUL/DEC)

Total: **$5,000.00** ($2,500.00)

- **Expenses Paid Annually:**
  - **Life Insurance Bob - 800** (Due JUL)
  - **Life Insurance Janet - 650** (Due NOV)
  - **Automobile Property Tax – 800** (Due OCT)
  - **Credit Cards & Amazon Prime Fees – 120** (0) (90, 30)
  - House Maintenance - 750 (240) (300, 150, 50,)
  - Car Maintenance – 750 (210) (50, 250, 100, 90)
  - Medical Costs – 3,000 (400) (150, 1,500, 800,)

Total: **$6,860.00** ($850.00)

Total Annual Recurring Expenses: **$13,260.00** ($3,350.00)

SECTION 4
Annual Travel

Annual Total: - $3,600.00 ($100.00) ()

SECTION 5
Monthly Income

- **Bob's Monthly Paycheck: $2,500.00**
- **Janet's Monthly Paycheck: $3,333.00**

Total Take Home Pay: $5,833.00

SECTION 6
Savings And Investments

- IRA – Bob - $62,000.00
- 401K Plan - Janet - $88,000.00
- Joint Savings Account – $6,500.00

TOTAL: $156,500.00

pay for Christmas gift expenses. This is a benefit of programming well and being thrifty.

The Annual Total for Section 4 is ($100), indicating that the annual travel budget is currently overspent by $100. Section 4 is a candidate for some cross-leveling of funds from other areas. Where would you take funds from to bring Travel back to (0)?

In Sections 5 & 6, Bob and Janet are already thinking about what to do with their upcoming pay raises for the new year. They are leaning toward leaving the budget as it is currently and putting any pay increases into their savings and investments which are deducted directly from their gross pay.

Bob and Janet have had a good budget year! How will yours be?

"Money grows on the tree of persistence."
– Japanese proverb

"Money is a guarantee that we may have what we want in the future. Though we need nothing at the moment, it ensures the possibility of satisfying a new desire when it arises." - Aristotle

Final Thoughts

My hope is that by the time you get to this point in the book you have already built your Budget Dashboard slide and are currently tinkering with your own annual spending plan and monthly budget. There are few things more empowering in this daunting world than controlling your own financial resources and maximizing their spending power to the greatest extent possible.

If you are not yet at that point, I urge you to set the time aside to build your Dashboard and begin to enjoy the financial control you deserve. After all, the only thing between you and financial management success is just a few clicks to create some frames and insert some text boxes, just like you probably have already done at school or at work. So go ahead, take the leap. You won't regret it.

I would also urge you to review all the wise money sayings which are quoted throughout the book to cheer you on in your efforts. The great people who shared these thoughts knew what they were saying and wanted you to gain this financial wisdom for your own benefit; otherwise they would have kept these ideas to themselves.

"Live long and prosper." – Mr. Spock

www.ingramcontent.com/pod-product-compliance
Lightning Source LLC
Chambersburg PA
CBHW051919210526
45473CB00006B/2073